Bride to Be

Bride to Be

Jacyln C. Hirschhaut & Kate Taylor
Illustrated by Robyn Neild

BARRON'S

First edition for the United States, its territories and dependencies published in 2006 by Barron's Educational Series, Inc.

All inquiries should be addressed to:
Barron's Educational Series, Inc.
250 Wireless Blvd.
Hauppauge, NY 11788
www.barronseduc.com

ISBN-13: 978-0-7641-3460-9
ISBN-10: 0-7641-3460-4

Library of Congress Control No.: 2005932388

Conceived and produced by
Elwin Street Limited
79 St John Street
London EC1M 4NR
www.elwinstreet.com

b13391136

Designer: Maura Fadden Rosenthal/Mspace
Illustrator: Robyn Neild

Printed and bound in Singapore.

9 8 7 6 5 4 3 2 1

contents

Introduction   7

introduction

"Congratulations! You're going to be a bride!"

Chances are, these words will have quite an effect on you—only it might not be the one that you most expect. Instead of feeling uplifted and excited, you are more likely feeling scared and a little bit shaky right now.

The truth is, planning a wedding is wonderful. It's also frightening, stressful and—no one will tell you this—capable of inducing neurotic thoughts in even the most calm bride to be. Typical panics that arise as the event approaches are that your fiancé might be run over the morning of the wedding and that you'll never manage to look prettier than your maid of honor. Of course, all such fears are unfounded: your fiancé will live to become your husband and the angels will conspire to give your maid of honor a bad-hair day (for which you will be eternally grateful).

So you should know by now that it is perfectly normal to become a little anxious as you plan the biggest day of your life, and this should prepare you for the fluctuating emotions you will experience over the months to come. You will be crazy about your fiancé one morning, only to find yourself mad at him that afternoon when he refuses to get excited about the flowers. You'll change your mind about your dress with alarming frequency, and you'll be resentful of anyone who cancels after you spent a month on the seating plan.

In spite of this emotional roller coaster, however, planning your wedding can be as easy, fulfilling, and as fun as you always imagined. The key is preparation—and this book. A godsend for brides, *Bride to Be* divides the entire wedding process into manageable sections, starting with the engagement right through to honeymoon ideas and the Big Day itself. You will find advice on everything from venues to vows, and will be able to indulge in every bridal fantasy you've ever had.

It is all here, and with our wealth of shared experience, all the resources we've gathered together, and your enthusiasm, you simply can't fail to plan the wedding of your dreams—even if your maid of honor simply refuses to have a bad-hair day.

Congratulations! You're going to be a bride! (And you're going to love it.)

Chapter One

You're Engaged!

Let's get this wedding party started. You're officially engaged. Congratulations! But you know only too well that the questions are already coming. Is it rude to reject his choice of ring if you hate it? Should you announce your engagement in the newspapers? Does anybody have engagement parties these days and, if so, who plays host? Relax. The engagement is the easiest part of the whole affair. It's a time for celebration, not agitation. Here's how to cope with effortless grace.

We've done it!

Dear Diary,

I am. . . engaged! Yes, it has finally happened. They said one day my prince would come and he has. John—handsome, wonderful John—finally got his knee dirty and asked me to marry him. And I said yes!

Actually I shouted "yes!" Or more specifically (and a million times more embarrassing) "Yes, please."

It all happened last week, as we walked back home in the rain from a party. I was a little bit drunk and was babbling on about something or other, paying no attention to how quiet John had become. Suddenly John is down on one knee, all serious, looking at me with such an open, honest expression of intent, affection, and panic. I'm sure he was thinking he was going to lose me forever unless he offered me what I wanted most: to share his future.

Beautiful moment, ruined by me suddenly asking, "Where's the ring?"

John's look of affection turned to panic, and he quietly said, "Thought we'd go look at rings together." Should have known my thoughtful guy would take that course of action. He is truly a prince; how bad did I feel?!

So I used to be right-handed: not any more. Since this platinum-and-diamond solitaire (princess cut, naturally) was installed on my ring finger, I'm finding I use my left hand for everything. Hailing a taxi? Up it goes, twinkling in the sunshine. Paying for stuff—my left hand waves the money in front of the vendor like I'm trying to hypnotize her.

Getting the ring was fabulous. J. came over to my apartment the night before, barely visible behind an armful of champagne and roses, and we spent a giggly evening discussing what kind of ring we'd like. Yes—WE'D like. I was surprised at how firm his views were. I'd always expected it to be completely my choice, that my future husband (whoever he'd be) would be happy for me to wear anything. It seems not. J. said he thought platinum and diamond would be best. I almost argued out of habit, until it sunk in. What? He's insisting I go for platinum and diamond? Oh, OK then. Twist my arm . . . The next day we went to 47th Street, hand in hand. After pressing our noses against ten windows, we realized that our budget wouldn't stretch to any of the wrist-breaking rocks. Several smaller, more delicate rings—with smaller, more delicate price tags—were affordable though, and I tried on everything until we found THE ring. I just knew. It was square, with chiseled edges, set in a platinum band. It looked exactly like a princess's ring—like a fairy-tale ring. It made me cry. And that sealed it.

Not having an engagement party. Is that boring? Have we already settled down to a nothing-happening life? Are we resigning ourselves to never having fun again? Or are we just Not Very Rich? Hmm. We're NVRs—sounds a lot like envious. I am getting very jealous of brides to be who have loads of cash to spend on wedding stuff. But then, I'm not jealous of their partners; nobody is as handsome and funny as J.

The ring

Did he propose and you cried out "yes!" . . . or did you propose and he accept? Whatever the circumstances of your engagement, the appearance of a ring on the fourth finger of your left hand will be the first sign that a wedding is in the works.

Traditionally, the groom gets the whole thing going by professing his love, offering a marriage proposal, and presenting a dazzling diamond ring. While the height of romance for some of us, this is not the only option. Perhaps, like our bride to be, your man proposed without a ring, insistent that you choose the jewelry you will wear daily for the rest of your life; or maybe one of you has a family ring. Other ideas are to shop for antique jewelry together or to seek one-of-a-kind designs.

For many couples, the engagement ring, or another item of jewelry, will be the most treasured—and expensive—wedding item on the list. Traditionally, the cost rests entirely with your fiancé, its price equal to about two months of his salary.

Buying together

Savvy shoppers will certainly do some homework first. Steer clear of jewelers promoting deep discounts, and take note of word-of-mouth recommendations. Long-standing, well-established jewelry stores are among the most reputable and are typically staffed by experienced sales personnel who can identify the finest jewels within a specified price range.

Choosing the stone

If you are buying jewelry, you should think about your choice of diamonds or colored gems, and if you want a diamond, you should start with four important diamond characteristics: cut, color, clarity, and carat.

The sparkle of your diamond is determined by its cut, or the arrangement of its 58 facets, which reflect light. A well-cut diamond sparkles more brilliantly than one of lesser quality.

A stone's color can range from clear to hues of blue, pink, or yellow. Clear is preferred by many, since color is thought to obstruct a stone's ability to reflect light.

Clarity refers to the tiny, natural flaws of a stone, which can only be seen under magnification. Diamonds containing the fewest of these "inclusions" are considered to be of the best clarity and command a higher price.

Finally, the weight of a stone is measured in carats and points, with 100 points equaling one carat. Typically, the carat weight is the least important consideration in assessing the value of a diamond; while the most important is whether you both love it!

The design

The design of any piece of jewelry you buy should reflect your sense of style and also suit your lifestyle. The metal and the shape of the setting should be chosen to enhance the gem. The simplest settings will show off a beautiful stone best. If either you or your fiancé has a special stone, a good jeweler will be able to design a new setting to flatter it. Remember, too, that if you have an engagement ring, after the wedding you also will most likely wear a wedding band. The band and your engagement jewelry aren't required to match, but you will probably want them to coordinate in fit, design, and color.

You'll want to take care of your new, prized possession, so you might want to secure a written appraisal of the stone and setting from your jeweler, and forward a copy to your insurance agent. Precious jewelry should be insured against loss, damage, or theft, and your insurance agent can add a rider to your home owner's policy to cover it. It's also a good idea to have your jewels cleaned and the settings checked every six months to keep them sparkling!

Other options

You don't have to have a ring to symbolize your commitment to each other. How about a simple diamond pendant or earrings? Nor do you have to have a piece of jewelry—just pick something that is special to the two of you.

Enjoying your engagement

You've formalized your commitment to one another. Once the shock wears off and you stop staring at the gorgeous ring on your finger, reality is going to hit with a THUD! Planning a wedding is a big job, but, before it takes over your life, make sure you enjoy the thrill of being engaged for as long as you can.

Stay on cloud 9

Hang on to that dreamy, heart-pounding feeling by keeping your engagement a secret for up to 48 hours. This will be hard, since you'll being dying to tell family and friends, but it will give you time for the reality of your decision to sink in. Once your head is out of the clouds, the first thing you should do is consider how long your engagement will be. An engagement usually lasts from six months to a year, but many couples don't stick to those parameters. It will depend on your ideal wedding date, how much time you need to prepare, and the availability of venues, and so on.

Doing battle

Once you've left cloud 9 and have told family and friends, the calls will start. Everyone will want to know if you've set a date, where you are going to get married, what you are going to wear, and on and on. It's easy to let this barrage of questions stress you out—but don't let it. If people keep pressuring you for answers, just tell them that once you've come off your cloud, they'll be the first to know all the details.

Getting started

After a few weeks of hopefully stress-free bliss, you should feel ready to get started. Don't wait too long to start planning, particularly since some venues, bands, caterers, and other essentials are booked a year or more in advance.

Announcements and parties

Announcing your engagement

Now that you've accepted his proposal (or he's accepted yours) and have told your family and closest friends, you can formally announce your intentions together. According to wedding etiquette, the groom's parents should contact the bride's parents first, to express their delight at the news. And, once your parents have exchanged courtesies, you can start to tell other family members and friends. Telephone calls and emails are acceptable methods for contacting most people, but you might want to send handwritten notes to older, more traditionally-minded relatives if you are unable to tell them in person.

Consider whether you want to announce your engagement in a newspaper. If either of you is living away from your hometown, it might be a good way of letting old school friends and neighbors know the good news.

Another option is to announce your engagement over the Internet. It is by far the quickest way of getting news to distant friends and relatives, and is a real break with tradition.

The engagement party

The party can be as formal or as informal as you wish, but there should always be a toast to the prospective newlyweds. Be prepared for guests bringing gifts of a practical household nature; you might want to make it clear whether you expect such gifts and deal swiftly with any necessary thank-yous.

"Stephen proposed to me in an email, which is typical of him, so it seemed fitting for us to tell everybody about our engagement over the Internet." Sophie, 31

Survival tactics

Whether you were expecting the proposal or not, it does not always follow that you knew how or where your fiancé was going to pop the question. Here are some hints on how to handle tricky situations:

Accepting a proposal

Your fiancé will have thought long and hard about how to propose, so spare a moment for how he must be feeling. Whatever you do, do not take too long to say "yes." Every second will seem like an eternity to him, and it's cruel to leave him hanging.

Rejecting a ring

What if your fiancé pops the question and presents you with a ring that you hate? The solution lies in honesty and tactfulness. You are going to have the ring for a long time and it should be one you are happy with. Look for something you do like about it and suggest changing other aspects to make it more "personal" to you.

The "ex" question

One of you is bound to have had a close relationship in the past, where you need to be particularly sensitive in breaking your news. In such cases it is best to call early on so that your ex does not hear it from someone else.

Keeping your head

Many couples will find themselves stressed out as they try to please everyone involved in their celebration. Learning the art of compromise early on is invaluable, as is relying on tried-and-true wedding etiquette to move beyond any sticky situations.

Resources

How to buy a diamond

The Diamond Registry
Tel: 800/223-7955
www.diamondregistry.com

Jewelers of America
Tel: 800/223-0673
www.jewelers.org

Gemological Institute of America (GIA)
Tel: 800/421-7250
www.gia.edu

Jewelry Information Center
Tel: 800/459-0130
www.jewelryinfo.org

U.S. Federal Trade Commission
Tel: 1-877/FTC-HELP
www.ftc.gov/bcp/conline/pubs/products/jewelry
Publication *All That Glitters: How to Buy Jewelry*
available by phone and online

Tiffany & Company
Tel: 800/843-3269
www.tiffany.com

www.debeers.com

www.adiamondisforever.com

www.diamondgrading.com

Choosing a jeweler

www.diamondreview.com

Designing your own ring

WeddingChannel.com
www.weddingchannel.com

www.thediamondbuyingguide.com

Antique and estate jewelry

www.antiqueandestate.com

Chapter Two

Your Wedding Theme

Ever wondered how some brides manage to have the most amazingly coordinated wedding day? It's all in the planning. Once you decide on your theme, you'll find it's suddenly easy to choose the right venue, dress, flowers, readings—everything—to harmonize beautifully. It's just a matter of knowing what you want. Grab a scrapbook and your imagination and start fantasizing about your Perfect Day.

My wedding theme

So excited. Today, Anita (bridesmaid) and I sat down to discuss My Wedding Theme. She thought I should go for something exotic like a sunset wedding on a big, gorgeous sailboat. And because I'm not your average looking girlie—with this shock of red hair and whiter-shade-of-snow skin—something on the wild side might not be such a bad idea.

Of course, this is not just about me. The theme should carry through to all areas of the wedding, from flowers to invitations to table settings to bridesmaids. This calls for major organization and a fortune's worth of bridal magazines.

LOVE bridal magazines. They're not the height of editorial creativity, but brides to be don't want that. What we want are a ton of pictures of brides, flowers, and castles, with features telling us how to look stunning for next to nothing. After a day's reading, have made following decisions:

Theme: Bride of Dracula

Description: dramatic dress, castle (or similar), J. in tails, blood-red roses, candelabras . . .

Where: somewhere in the valley (near my parents)

Bridesmaids: A. and Becky (J.'s niece)

My hair: up, with hanging curls

Invitations: equally dramatic—handmade paper, copper-plate writing, black card

Wedding car: stretch limo

Yes, I know the limo doesn't really go with the theme, but they're my favorite cars and I always wanted one. Ideally (a word I find I use eight times a day lately), the reception would be held outdoors, with a perfect table setting—snowy-white tablecloths billowing, candelabras dripping—on the lawn. Like an outdoor dinner party. It'd be so dramatic and fabulous. So original and different. So memorable and . . .

"Cold," said Mom. "And maybe wet and definitely hard to arrange. Why on earth can't you go for something practical?"

AARGH! It's my wedding. MY special day. Why can't she just be pleased and supportive? Tried to fume for hours after that phone call but found I couldn't, as slightly agreed with her point. It would be a shame if it rained—it'd be ruined. And maybe burning candles and billowing tablecloths weren't ideal tablemates.

Decided to tone it down. To keep the "dramatic" theme, maybe J. and I could marry in a country hotel? With beautiful grounds and big dining hall. I could wear long gorgeous dress, he could be in tails, and we could have ivy and roses twining everywhere. Anyway, am seeing J. tomorrow so will discuss.

Stupid men! Interfering b*&%$*s! All I got from J. was a stunned silence, then hysterical laughter. He thought it was the stupidest thing he'd ever heard. Has he NO imagination? OK, maybe the Dracula bit is a little nuts, but you have to start crazy and tone it down. Otherwise it just gets boring.

He has always wanted a small, quiet wedding in the country. Who knew? Who would have thought men plan things like that? He pictured me in a simple white dress and a reception over-looking rolling hills. He wants simple and small; I want dra-matic and memorable. He says "tomato" and I say "ugh, salad." He likes minimalism, I like to pull out all the stops. Let's call the whole thing off. . .

It's going to have to be a compromise, and that worries me. Do not want to "settle" on wedding day. Too important. Marriage is something you only do, ooh, four times in your life, so want to do it right.

But, actually. . . after a chat, there are things that J. and I do agree on. Like the country thing. That was in my vision too, so we can work on that. And he does want to wear something that will make him look—and feel—like a hero from a romantic novel. It's going to HAVE to be simple and small because our budget is, well, tiny. And maybe the castle is a bit too Madonna and Guy Ritchie. Need to think. But this proves that the engagement stage is important—learning to accommodate each other's dreams and wishes to get something we both want.

But I'll miss Dracula. That would've been so cool.

Where to start

It is perfectly normal to have mixed feelings about planning your wedding, especially since there seems to be so much that needs doing right from day one. Don't be like our bride to be. . . the best place to start is by talking to your fiancé about the style of wedding you both would like and taking notes on all of your ideas.

First, think about what's most important to the two of you and make lists of the various elements that would make the day perfect, from the obvious through to your wildest dreams. Remember, this is a chance to express your personal style. Pinpoint areas you won't budge on as well as aspects where you can be flexible. Begin a realistic conversation about financing the wedding and where the money to cover the expenses will come from. Set up a time to speak with each of your families to determine if they can contribute to the budget.

As you begin to firm up your decisions, it may become apparent that you have to compromise along the way; one decision often impacts another and you will need to adapt accordingly. It is important for you to be prepared to make adjustments while still keeping your priorities in focus.

When to get married

Similar to planning any other type of special event, the simplest plans require the shortest time in arranging, while more elaborate celebrations with fine-tuned details will demand more time and more money.

Organizing a wedding celebration typically spans at least six months to a year or more. At the beginning, it may seem like an inordinate amount of time is spent in making preparations for an event that primarily lasts just one day. But, with the help of both your families, your closest friends, and a flurry of professionals, you will soon get into it. Be realistic about the amount of time you'll need for shopping and setting up the arrangements, and build in a cushion of an extra week or so. If your time is short or you have extra money, consider hiring a professional wedding planner to guide you through the process (see page 28).

Weddings take place during every month of the year, and you'll want to consider when the weather will be ideal and guests can travel to the location easily.

Selecting the day itself is sometimes the result of coordinating your families' schedules with the availability of the professionals and the venue you want to hire. All facilities and party professionals are in higher demand at certain times of the year—notably the spring and summer months—and are busier on certain days over others, namely Saturdays. Having a little flexibility within your desired time frame might allow money savings and assure that fulfilling your dream is less complicated.

Furthermore, the last thing that you would want to experience is that you're both so exhausted from planning all the details that you can't be rested, relaxed, and ready to thoroughly enjoy the time surrounding your wedding day. So avoid scheduling your wedding at a time that's expected to be busy for you or your fiancé, and away from other family commitments or major projects at work.

Choosing a theme

Whether or not you have fantasized about your wedding day when you were a little girl, you probably remember playing "dress up" to a fairy-tale wedding story, wearing a sparkling ball gown and a princess tiara, and your handsome prince riding onto the scene on the most magnificent horse.

Fast-forward to today, and your image of you and your fiancé may well have a very different look to it. However, this does not mean there cannot be a sense of enchantment surrounding your wedding celebrations. Big or small, country or city, every wedding takes on a style that is tied to the bride and groom and their own dreams of how their day should be.

More often than not, a theme will evolve from the season in which you wed; think about the stunning flowers that can inspire a spring—or summertime—wedding, while the vivid foliage of fall is ideal for the cooler months. And what better inspiration for an all-white theme than a perfect winter wonderland setting? Other sources for inspiration might include bygone eras, a movie, a fairy tale, the honeymoon destination, and the location of the ceremony and reception.

Making it unique

When it comes to saying your vows, the surroundings you choose can be as familiar as your own home, your neighborhood church or synagogue, a nearby landmark, or an exotic destination.

Similarly, the invitations, decorations, music, food, and drink can be chosen to complement the basic theme of your wedding and reflect your personal style as a couple. Remember, too, that the guests who witness your wedding are an especially vital ingredient, and many of the special touches can be chosen primarily with them in mind.

The following are some ideas on how to use a central theme and tie in various aspects of your wedding:

- In a garden or casual setting, consider a country-style wedding with invitations printed on handmade paper with pressed flowers. Arrange the bridesmaids' bouquets in baskets and base the reception on a simple buffet of your favorite summer foods. Drape the dining tables in floral or checkered cloths decked with eyelet-trimmed napkins, and place a miniature vase of cut flowers at each setting. Where folk music and traditional dancing is part of the entertainment, offer seed packets to guests as they leave the reception.

- For a super-cool, cold-weather wedding, create a winter wonderland by filling the setting with numerous ivory candles in hurricane sleeves and votives. Decorate small trees in tiny twinkling lights to frame the site or set dry ice in water to create a cloudlike stage. Pass cups of steaming, hot mulled cider or wine as guests arrive at the reception.

- Focus on your favorite color for a design theme, introduced first in the envelope sleeve of your wedding invitation. Choose a complementary tone for the bridesmaids' gowns and the mothers' corsages. Fill your ceremony and reception venues with flowers, balloons, or candles in coordinated colored tones. Dress the reception chairs in loose fabric covers, and trim favors for the guests with matching ribbon.

- Schedule your wedding near a holiday, especially Christmas or Valentine's Day, and you'll have an automatic theme to work around.

In a tropical setting, decorate with vivid citrus colors of orange, yellow, and lime. Fill the venue with native flowers, trees, and palm fronds. Choose a menu of grilled foods and decorate the plates with edible petals. Serve fruity drinks inspired by the local habitat and seal the ambience with music from a steel drum band.

"I thought Michael was joking when he said he wanted to get married in Hawaii. It sounded so out of our reach. But we found a company that took care of all the arrangements... All the bridesmaids wore grass skirts and the groomsmen leis. Cheesy maybe, but I would do it again tomorrow." **Julia 27**

The guest list

For some couples, a wedding just wouldn't be a wedding without a large crowd of friends and relatives. For others, a purposefully small wedding party is preferred. The choice is influenced by the budget as well as the capacity of the ceremony and reception venues.

The wedding party

The wedding party will comprise favorite family members and friends who surround the two of you on the day, contributing to the unfolding events:

- The maid of honor is, traditionally, the bride's closest unmarried friend, often her sister, and the matron of honor is her closest married friend or relative. She is usually the last bridesmaid in the wedding procession, and during the ceremony she holds the bride's bouquet and arranges the bride's veil and train as necessary.

- The bridesmaids can be the sisters, cousins, and friends of the bride who support her during the engagement. They usually precede her as she walks up the aisle.

- The father of the bride traditionally "gives" her in marriage, although the duty can also be handled by both parents, a stepfather, brother, uncle, or close family friend. However, the bride doesn't have to be "given" away, and some couples prefer to walk up the aisle together.

- The mother of the bride is distinguished as the last guest to be seated for the ceremony and is considered the official hostess of the wedding reception.

- The best man is the groom's best friend or relative who stands up front with him as the marriage ceremony begins, and who is responsible for delivering the rings at the ceremony and acting as an usher, if necessary.

- The groomsmen support the groom during the engagement and bring him to the wedding.

- Many weddings include young children in the wedding party: a ring bearer might carry a pillow on which symbolic wedding rings are tied, while a flower girl might scatter flower petals in the bride's path.

Choosing your bridesmaids

Your most likely choice for bridesmaids will be your sisters and/or your best friends. They may also be chosen from members of your fiancé's family. But don't feel obliged to ask a friend or relative just because you were a bridesmaid at their wedding.

The invitation to be a bridesmaid is one a girl either relishes or dreads. For some it is a dream come true and there is nothing they wouldn't do to support a true friend. For others, the fear of having to wear some monstrous outfit overrides the pleasure of being selected. Try to anticipate the reactions of your chosen few and be prepared to dispel/instill enthusiasm accordingly.

Since being a bridesmaid requires a substantial financial commitment to cover the cost of an outfit, travel expenses, participating in and planning your bachelorette party, and choosing a wedding gift, you should make sure she's comfortable with her role. If not, give her the opportunity to take another role at the wedding, such as presenting a reading during the service.

One of the big challenges will be keeping everyone informed of the details as the wedding plans fall into place. Keep your bridesmaids updated on pre-wedding parties and the rehearsal, and let the unattached ones know about any single guys who will be there on the day.

Make it special

Think of ways to reward your bridesmaids for their spirited devotion to your cause!

- Book appointments for manicures and pedicures together.
- Treat them to a special lunch or brunch on the day before the wedding.
- Present each one with a gift, along with a note of how important her friendship and help have been during your engagement.
- Make time to speak personally with each bridesmaid on your wedding day.
- Send a postcard to each attendant while you are on your honeymoon.
- Once you return, make plans to get together for a girls' night out.

Do you need a wedding planner?

So many details . . . so little time! Exactly how much time do you have to plan your marriage ceremony and the reception that will follow? For a growing number of couples, the help of a professional wedding planner is a surprisingly cost-effective service that can take your ideas and turn them into reality.

Even the simplest wedding celebration requires countless hours of careful planning and dedicated attention to a vast number of details. Not only will you need help in choosing the right wedding specialists for the day, but you'll also want to avoid making potentially embarrassing mistakes. A planner can become your best friend as you work together to take the effort out of creating the perfect wedding.

There are times when the services of a professional are especially helpful to the bride and groom; for example, if you are planning a long-distance wedding, or if either of your parents are divorced and you need neutral advice on how to accommodate the extra opinions and satisfy their needs under pressure. Similarly, when keeping to a budget is a high priority, a wedding planner can advise on spending wisely and steering clear of costly mistakes. He or she can also help to negotiate the contracts with the service providers, making sure that no detail is forgotten.

And, of course, a wedding planner is the obvious option if you are reluctant to handle the inevitable mountain of telephone calls and appointments yourself and want to avoid facing difficult questions and challenging dilemmas. You will be able to relax completely on your wedding day, confident that any last-minute crisis will be expertly handled by someone else!

Hiring a wedding planner

While some couples hire planners to handle the entire event, others sign them up to take over specific assignments. Obviously, the decision is usually dependent upon the budget. Professional wedding planners can be paid by the hour or they can charge an agreed-upon percentage of the fees from the caterer, florist, and musicians that they book on your behalf. The relationship between the couple and the planner should be settled at the first meeting—and before any planning begins.

The preferable approach to finding a wedding planner is by word of mouth. If you have a friend or relative who raves about the service they got, snap up the phone number. Otherwise, look out for advertisements and listings in bridal magazines.

The budget

If you haven't done so already, now is the time for you and your fiancé to sit down and set a budget. The cost of a wedding is dependent upon one factor: time. The more time you have to shop around, the more money you could save.

On the other hand, if you want to be married sooner rather than later, you'll most likely grab details of the wedding that appeals to the two of you as soon as you find them, regardless of the price tag. But by drawing up a budget, you will accomplish two objectives. First, it will help to provide a realistic plan for how much money you will need. Second, by listing all the elements separately, you will provide yourself with a checklist, which can then be arranged in terms of priority and/or cost.

Start by compiling two lists: essentials and desirables—and get a good balance of both. Do some research to get an initial idea of likely costs, bearing in mind that the more formal the wedding, the more expensive it will be. There is always the possibility that you will go over budget on some areas of planning, and you should have a contigency plan for dealing with this.

Survival tactics

Make the right choices now and you will avoid unnecessary complications as your plans develop. The two key areas are communication and budget; you and your fiancé should know the direction you are going in from the start, and keep a close eye on your finances.

Don't forget your fiancé!

It's all too easy for a bride to get wrapped up in her own grand plan, almost completely forgetting to consider her fiancé's vision of the Big Day. There are aspects that he will want to have input in, so be sensitive to including him in making those decisions.

Don't overdo it

While there is no doubt that it is the sum of all the details that will create the day of your dreams, there's a real danger of going way overboard in your eagerness to create the "perfect" wedding. Rather than trying to have a little of everything, concentrate on a few key elements for maximum style.

Tips for saving money

The most obvious consideration is the size of the guest list. For couples with limited funds, think about hosting a small wedding with your immediate family and closest friends, and having a special party for your larger circle of friends at a later date.

The scheduling of your wedding can have a direct effect on costs. You could choose to be married on a Sunday afternoon to avoid the premiums placed on Saturday affairs, or opt for a daytime celebration rather than an evening one.

If you can't afford a wedding planner, enlist the help of family and friends to help out with simple, but laborious tasks.

Resources

Theme weddings

Fairytale Wedding Shop
Tel: 888/9-SHELLS
www.fairytaleweddingshop.com

Fantasea Weddings
Tel: 866/326-8273
www.fantaseaweddings.com

The Knot.com
Tel: 1-877/THE-KNOT
www.theknot.com

Theme Works Productions
Tel: 760/288-4924
www.themeworksproductions.com

WeddingChannel.com
Tel: 888/750-1550
www.weddingchannel.com

WeddingDetails.com
Tel: 888/968-5565
www.weddingdetails.com

Wedding Gazette
www.weddinggazette.com

Your Wedding Company
Tel: 206/241-8224
www.yourweddingcompany.com

www.countryweddings.com

www.day2remember.com

www.foreverwed1.com

www.todays-weddings.com

www.usabride.com

Destination weddings

www.disney.go.com

www.resortvacationstogo.com

Ethnic weddings

www.askginka.com

Chapter Three

Choosing The Venue

Choosing where to get married may be the main decision you and your fiancé will have to make. Not only do you have to decide whether to have a religious or civil ceremony, but wherever you host the reception has to be accommodating, available, affordable, and needs to fit in with your wedding theme. These days you are allowed to get married almost anywhere, from castle to cabin cruiser. You could rent a movie theater and be the main feature. Your groom could say his vows from the bow of a ship. You could fly to Antigua, Italy, Morocco . . .

Choosing the venue

I am so tired—fell asleep on the train this morning. Up all night celebrating my betrothal in all manner of exotic, double-jointed ways. If only. In fact, sex has left the building. J. and I haven't so much as brushed past each other for the last— Oh My God—five days. I think it's because we've been seeing so much of my parents.

Great weekend. J. took us to five different venues to check out wedding facilities. We agreed on which we liked best too, which was a blessing. It is gorgeous—attached to a vineyard, with stunning grounds, and we get to hold the reception in a huge old stable. They've got rooms for people to stay in, too, which is handy for some of our longer-distance guests. Not sure if we'll stay there, though—J. says he hasn't thought that far ahead yet!

So we've booked it tentatively—have even chosen a date. Gulp! Having a fixed date really brings it all home. But will be good to have a day to tell people. Whenever have to say, "No, we haven't finalized the date yet," I always feel that what they hear is, "No, I can't pin him down to commitment at all. He clearly doesn't love me."

Arranged second viewing of venue with Mom and Dad for next weekend. Mom excited, Dad a bit too. Me? Guilty for taking up J.'s weekends with wedding stuff. (Stupid, as is his wedding, too.) Think I need early night. Am getting very paranoid.

It's booked! And secured. Dad has paid a deposit. So excited. Looked even better this time round, and J. looked very proud of self for finding it. Mom got misty-eyed as we looked at the huge, old-beamed stable where the ceremony will take place. There are huge gardens rolling down to river. Swank-central. And a massive bar. Bliss, because I think I'll need a gallon of champagne on Big Day.

The hotel gave us loads of stuff to take home, so I now have official Wedding File started. Feel organized at last. Plus, can finally start thinking about dress design, too, now know setting. The vineyard is very old, so could go for big, dramatic number. Wish I'd gone for winter wedding now, so could have worn velvet and fake fur. But then I'd have been getting married in less than six months . . . so maybe I don't . . .

Of course, even though venue has been chosen, no reason to stop viewings altogether. They are very fun way of getting to snoop around hotels and get coffee and cookies free. So Jules (old roommate) and I called up some more hotels and arranged "viewings." Was her idea. I had no part in it . . . Except I was the bride and had to do most talking. It was fun, but scary since she had booked us into the fanciest hotels she could think of.

At one place I think we were busted immediately. Jules asked to see the honeymoon suite and ran right into it, opening mini bar and getting in bathtub. So embarrassing. I had to distract man showing us around by asking grown-up questions about parking facilities and availability. Meanwhile Jules is hopping around behind man, mouthing, "I have stolen the champagne—it's in my purse." Hysterical. Man started to get rude when I got giggles, so Jules announced that somewhere else had better tea and coffee making facilities and dragged me out. Doubled over with laughter. Am sure will be put on hotel's "most wanted" list of people never to accept bookings from.

Told J. about it later and was sure he'd think it was funny. Was surprised: he was on a downer. Asked him why. OK, bugged him until he caved in and told me why. He was having worries that he'd never be able to keep me in high style. Said that when he saw me in all those hotels he realized that I loved them, but that he'd never be able to take me away to fancy places like that. He was upset.

Can't he see that it's him I want, not a lifestyle? No amount of free Aveda soap and mini bars could replace what I've found in him: laughter, love, and lust. All in one person. Tried to explain that, but came out all wrong, so showed him instead.

The art of compromise

Once caught up in the flurry of planning a wedding, it is easy to lose sight of the fact that the single most important event of the day is the ceremony itself. Long after the last petal is tossed, the bottom line is that you and your fiancé will have become legally, physically, and emotionally bound to each other.

Whether you choose to be married in a house of worship or a civil option, your ceremony should be spiritual—a reflection of your love and dedication to each other. This spirituality can be captured as much by the traditions of your own faith, as it can by the roles of those who contribute on the day. So give thought to what will be said and who will be saying it.

For couples who share the same faith, there is a tendency to follow a set pattern, usually established by the religion in question. This does not have to be the case, however, and even the most traditional marriage ceremony can have personalized vows, readings, music, and decorations.

The best of both worlds

When planning an interfaith wedding, be careful to incorporate customs and traditions from both sides. This will help each family feel included and should avoid any impression of being left out.

If your marriage ceremony is to include two officiants and a blend of religious rites, be careful not to get caught up in the preferences of your respective cultures and families, or you will find yourselves having to make compromises in order to satisfy everyone. The savvy couple to be will become conciliators, making an effort to include future in-laws in the wedding plans, listening to their thoughts, and responding with simple adaptations to the wedding plans.

> "Jeff was raised in a small Pentecostal community and my parents are staunch Catholics, so we knew that our marriage would need to be discussed with sensitivity. After much discussion our officiants agreed to a ceremony that blended different aspects of our two faiths." Juliette, 37

Choice of ceremony

Once the two of you have decided whether you want a religious or secular service, it's time to determine where and when the ceremony will take place, and who will be officiating for you.

While there is something undoubtedly special about an outdoor wedding ceremony, the right weather cannot be guaranteed, and so more couples—like our bride and groom to be—opt for the ultimate control of an indoor site.

Religious ceremonies

The two of you can choose whether to be married in a chapel, church, or synagogue—yours, his, the one that either of you belonged to when growing up, or a neutral site. Since the marriage ceremony is the main event of the wedding celebration, you'll want to book the site ASAP.

Ask your clergy member or rabbi to help you schedule the wedding to avoid religious holidays. Consider the month, the day of the week, and the time of day in terms of tradition, ease of traveling to the desired location, and your budget.

Ideally, the officiant will be someone who has a personal relationship to you or your groom; he or she may be your family clergy member. In the event that you don't know the celebrant well, you should verify his or her credentials to be sure that they are properly licensed and authorized.

Couples of different faiths may choose to invite each of their respected officiants to perform the ceremony together, or they may conduct two separate services.

Every house of worship has its own procedures for being married, which may well include a requirement for pre-marriage counseling (see pages 102-103). Find out what this involves in order to allow enough time to complete the classes.

Second (religious) marriages

Special considerations may be necessary if either one of you has been married before. You will need to comply with the precepts of the faith as dictated by the clergy member. Some denominations do not consent to the conduct of a second wedding, while others may mandate special premarital counseling.

The ceremony at a second wedding is typically simple, with family members and close friends in attendance. Usually, the wedding party consists of just one attendant each and may include any children that the couple has. Depending on the layout of the location, the couple and their attendants take their place at the foot of the altar without the additional processional or giving away of the bride.

Civil ceremonies

A civil ceremony is probably the right choice for you if resolving differences of faith proves too great, if neither one of you is especially religious, or if either of you has been married before. While the essence of the union will be secular, some celebrants may allow you to integrate the odd traditional wedding rite into the service.

The most straightforward civil ceremony involves heading to a registry office and saying "I do" in front of a celebrant and witnesses. But, just for a moment, imagine yourself stepping down the grand staircase of a turn-of-the-century mansion or exchanging vows in a picturesque garden, or on the porch of a charming country inn. Or, say you have always dreamed of being wed on a sun-drenched beach or halfway up a mountain; anything is possible!

Choosing an unusual location, other than a house of worship for your marriage ceremony, can supply the perfect ambience for your once-in-a-lifetime wedding celebration, whether the place is stately and elegant or relaxed and casual. The real beauty of this type of wedding is that it enables you to arrange both the ceremony and reception in adjacent venues, cutting down on transportation and maximizing the time spent partying!

Consider the vast number of alternative locations to choose from: hotels, resorts, public gardens, parks, and also museums, theaters, and landmark buildings. Many of these kinds of locations will have their own coordinator for such an occasion—somebody to work with in organizing the day's events. Although you will ultimately be responsible for any arrangements made, the coordinator can divulge the details of previous successful weddings at the site and point out any of the venue's restrictions or limitations. He or she might also have photographs of weddings for ideas, and references from other couples who have used the venue in the past.

As with every major aspect of your wedding, you'll want to enter into a contract with the venue, outlining the services that will be provided to you as well as your responsibilities.

"Tom and I wanted our wedding day to be special, but not religious or municipal. When the registrar told us we could marry in our favorite bar, we jumped at the chance." Kate, 40

A wedding in paradise

Have you ever dreamed of being married in a tropical setting, where your wedding and honeymoon can be rolled into one glorious adventure? One-stop shopping for a destination wedding might be the answer and is some of the simplest wedding planning around.

Destination weddings are not limited to tropical locations; country inns, lakeside resorts, and mountain lodges are equally charming settings. The best hotels and inns have wedding consultants on site to take care of arrangements. They will organize food, hire musicians and a photographer, and specify the decorations and bouquets. You can have help picking out the perfect spot for the ceremony outside, with provisions made for an unexpected downpour. You can choose between an impressive garden, a picturesque lake, a breath-taking waterfall, or a quiet point along the ocean shore. . .

Most brides bring their own dress, but the groom can rent his attire on location. You could incorporate some of the local flavor in your accessories.

What do you need to know?

Choosing a venue in another state or foreign country can add a unique and significant flavor to your wedding celebration, but make sure that all local requirements are met. Check with the authorities at home as to whether they, too, have legal requirements.

The tourist bureau of the destination state or country is the primary source of necessary documentation. In addition to a passport, some foreign locations require a visa and specific inoculations. The most important detail in planning a wedding abroad is to allow enough time for the processing of all necessary paperwork.

Passport applications can usually be filed at the post office. For each application you must provide proof of citizenship, two passport photographs, a completed application form, and your payment. A visa is obtained by sending an application to the consulate of the destination country, along with both your passports.

Words and music

Once you have decided between a religious or civil ceremony, the next step is to find the words and music that best suit the occasion, and which reflect the personalities of both you and your fiancé.

Religious ceremonies may be marked with scripture readings, communion, or the lighting of a unity candle; civil ceremonies with readings of a non-religious nature. The most significant part of any ceremony, however, is the exchanging of vows. If religious, you may decide to follow your faith's prayer book, but this is also a chance to create meaningful vows of your own.

The music you choose will also be a key component of your wedding theme. Some of your selections will have significance for you as a couple, while others should mark specific events during the day.

Survival tactics

It may be fun to hold the celebrations at your favorite art museum, but make sure it has everything you need before you commit yourself to a booking:

Is it legal?

Ask the wedding coordinator about the legal requirements of being married at the site. And check state marriage laws if you're getting wed out of state.

Can it cater to all your needs?

Will you have exclusive rights to the entire location? Is it suitable for children? Are there adequate parking, coatroom, and rest room facilities? Finding answers to these and other questions at an early stage can avoid frustrations further down the line.

Get it in writing

As with every major aspect of your wedding, you'll want to enter into a contract with the venue, outlining the services that will be provided to you, as well as your responsibilities.

Troublesome guests

Extended families that result from divorced parents can add an element of stress. Identify issues of concern—though don't get involved in the politics—and plan accordingly. One solution for harmony on the wedding day is to be sure each parent is accompanied by a few of their close friends who can serve as allies to boost their morale.

Resources

Ceremony sites

The Knot.com
Tel: 1-877/THE-KNOT
www.theknot.com

National Garden Clubs
Tel: 314/776-7574
www.gardenclub.org

The Perfect Wedding Guide, Inc.
Tel: 888/222-7433
www.thepwg.com

WeddingChannel.com
Tel: 888/750-1550
www.weddingchannel.com

WeddingLocation.com
Tel: 800/933-3434
www.weddinglocation.com

www.topweddinglinks.com

Cruise weddings

www.theweddingexperience.com

www.royalwed.com

Destination weddings

Ever After
Tel: 651/246-6838
www.everafterwedding.com

Hawaii Visitors and Conventions Bureau
Tel: 800/GoHawaii (800/464-2924)
www.gohawaii.com

Romantic Beginnings
Tel: 203/795-8687
www.romanticbeginnings.com

VEGAS.com
Tel: 702/992-7900
www.vegas.com

www.weddings-abroad.com

Chapter Four

Planning The Reception

Party girls, get ready! Here's how to plan the biggest social event of the decade. The reception is the key to a perfect wedding day. It's where you get to indulge in every flight of fancy you ever dreamed of, from arriving in a Rolls Royce to dancing amid heart-shaped ice sculptures. Want something so fabulous that people are still talking about it in 20 years? Here's where you'll find ideas for the ultimate wedding-day showstoppers.

Dear Diary,

The reception

It's really starting to happen. Feelings: yay and eek. Vineyard people have been very helpful about reception style. And the freebies just keep coming. Jules told me you can get champagne-tastings and hors d'oeuvre samples and—you can! But got to stop. Am going to be huge before the (very) Big Day if do not get control of appetite.

Accomplished so far:

Flowers

Met fabulous florist, recommended by hotel, last week. Her portfolio was amazing—she has done flowers for famous people, as well as wedding scenes in movies.

J. loved meeting her since, with his gardening knowledge, he could spout Latin names all over place. It was very easy to decide, once we'd seen a few pictures. It's going to be roses and ivy. Ivy all over stables, along ceiling and edge of tables, and so on, with roses for bouquets, boutonnieres, and centerpieces.

Bit embarrassing when she asked me about my bouquet. My only opinion on this, previously (forgetting the embarrassing Dracula theme), had been that I didn't want one. Not really a very flowery person. But she understood, and we decided that it could look like these were just an armful of roses I'd picked on way to wedding. Like an innocent country girl. Quite like that picture of me. Better than a smoke-ridden, old city gal, anyway.

Table decorations

Center of tables: square glass vase filled with pebbles, with a single orchid. HOW chic? Florist had one in corner of her apartment and J. and I both loved it. And the pebble theme is really taking off: am going to have pebbles with guest's names painted on, as name cards. Rest of table will be simple elegance. Organizers have lots of little candles and holders we can use, so should be like twinkly grotto.

Food

Easy—we both picked our favorite meals. Lamb shank with mashed potatoes for me, salmon en croute for J. Two desserts: mini raspberry pavlova, and some chocolate cake thing that J. chose. Starters—pasta in pink sauce. Going to be SO delicious.

Dad also was total hero and arranged for us to have constantly circulating trays of hors d'oeuvres. Said he was sick of going to weddings where there's no food for hours.

Drinks

Vineyard wine REALLY expensive. Not much cheaper to bring our own, since they charge corkage on every bottle. But anyway, we don't have to choose very wide selection since there is cash bar there, too. (Don't mind that—I've never resented paying for my own drinks at a wedding, as long as wine is free with meal. And there are men to buy me drinks. And a mini bar in my room.)

So, it's champagne and champagne and orange juice as we arrive. Then red and white for meal, champagne for toasts, and a bottle of cognac on every table for speeches. Oh, and cigars for the men.

Music

This was embarrassing, but J. and I both want cheesy wedding disco. Like ones used to have when went to cousins' weddings as teenagers. The sort that play "Come on Eileen" to get everyone going, and "Lady In Red" to get everyone . . . er, really going. Vineyard representative swallowed a look of horror when we told him. But gave us a list and J. made two calls and sorted it. DJ has even agreed to wear his worst Seventies polyester suit to get even more cheesy. He'll start his set at 7:00 P.M., and end at midnight. Pleased it's a late one: want guests to have a good time at my wedding. Want lots of flirting and loads of gossip going on. (Maybe even babies made.)

Running order

Traditional. None of that modern "speeches before the meal" stuff. Everyone sits down at their places, J. and I get announced and waltz in, we eat, then speeches, then coffee and cake. It was good enough for our parents . . .

it's all in the planning

The reception is likely to be the first time you unwind from all the tensions of the previous few days, weeks, and months. Careful organization of this part of the wedding is essential if you are going to fully relax and enjoy yourself on the Big Day.

Since it follows directly after the marriage ceremony, the style of the reception should complement and reflect your wedding theme as closely as possible. Typically, the costs involved for the reception represent about half the entire wedding budget. And while, traditionally, the financial responsibility for the reception falls to the parents of the bride, it is not unusual for couples to receive assistance from the groom's family as well, or to assume some or all of the expenses themselves.

Wedding receptions can vary in style, size, and location. Yours can be as simple as walking from the place of worship to a fellowship hall that's been decorated for the occasion, or as elaborate as traveling to a nearby setting, where a team of professional staff are at hand to execute the party of a lifetime. A private club or favorite restaurant might offer the feeling of being at home without any of the hassles, while a swanky hotel has the added convenience of accommodations for out-of-town guests and the exhausted happy couple.

After you confirm the availability of your chosen reception site by signing a contract and submitting a deposit, it's time to roll up your sleeves and get on with the details. . .

Transportation

One of the last worries you'll want to have on your wedding day is that one of the bridesmaids can't find your house, or that a few of the groom's attendants got lost between the ceremony and the reception.

With a little pre-planning of wedding day transportation, you can be sure that all of the wedding party are exactly where they need to be and on time. Your budget may allow for a fleet of limousines to carry everyone from place to place. If not, think about friends, or friends of friends, who drive large cars or minivans and who might be willing to play chauffeur for you. Or do you know of a vintage car that might be available to you? Or what about a horse and carriage?!

Sit down with your fiancé and write the following lists to make sure that everyone in the wedding party is catered to: your pick-up location and time, plus the list of passengers who will ride with you to the ceremony; the groom's pick-up location and time, plus the list of passengers who will ride with him to the ceremony; and the location of the ceremony and time to depart for the reception, plus the list of all the VIPs who need transportation.

All out-of-town guests should be provided with maps and directions to all of the key wedding spots. You could ask family and friends to escort guests who aren't familiar with the area.

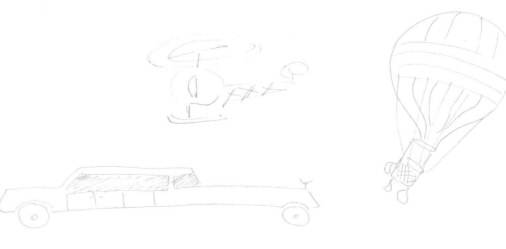

Wedding flowers

With about ten percent of the wedding budget allocated to flowers, it's important to secure a florist you can relate to—someone who understands what you want and who can work to your budget. Seek recommendations, and interview each candidate to determine who has the creative flair that works for you.

It is most practical to start with your dress and those of your bridesmaids as a basis for color scheme and style. Your bouquet should be considered an accessory to your dress, so not too enormous and not too tiny. The style of your dress will also influence what type of bouquet would look best or determine if a single flower would create a more dramatic image.

An established florist can advise how floral accents can enhance the setting. Most religious buildings require very little decoration beyond simple arrangements at the altar and on the pews for the family and wedding party. Some brides marrying in Jewish ceremonies will choose a *chuppah*, or wedding canopy, embellished with flowers. Check at the church or synagogue to learn of any guidelines or restrictions related to the decorations.

At the reception, flowers can be used to trim the surroundings as well as to enhance the table settings. You could have a small vase at each place setting, or place a larger arrangement at the center of the table. Be sure that the height of any centerpiece is either below or above the eye level of the guests around the table so as not to obstruct views or conversation.

Things to think about: which flowers will be in season when you get married; whether you would like any of the blooms to be scented; and whether you can save money by transferring the flowers from the ceremony to the reception. (Your florist may be able to do this for you.)

Something different

Go wild with your floral arrangements: garlands and displays made of foliage, woody stems, and berries can be striking; combine flowers with beads, candles, or pebbles (like our bride to be) to complement your theme; opt for bonsai or cacti for a super-stylish affair; and use fruit and vegetables, such as artichokes, pumpkins, and citrus fruit, for dramatic effect in the fall.

Wedding music

There is no limit to the music you can have at the reception—except, perhaps, space. Choose the music for your reception well and you will create the perfect ambience, and provide a vehicle for the entertainment.

Often, the size of the audience determines the best type of music, with a small ensemble best suited for a more intimate gathering and a mini-orchestra for a larger crowd. Another option that works best all around is a DJ who plays a selection of your favorite records, be they cheesy or achingly hip.

To begin planning live music for your reception, start by planning your budget and research the bands or musicians that fit in with your scheme. Next, assess the size and layout of the venue to establish the level of sound that is necessary to entertain the guests, but not overpower the festivities.

Ask around for recommendations from people who have hired or heard reception musicians, and who are also familiar with your tastes and style. Look for professionals who have ample experience, and who can relate to your vision of the party. Try to ascertain each band's depth of musical repertoire and their flexibility in satisfying any special requests.

Once you have selected the musical group for your reception, make plans to collaborate on the list of song titles to be played. Provide them with the date and time of the event, an agenda of the reception events, along with the number of musicians you want, appropriate attire, the fee, and the arrangement for overtime.

If you are sticking with tradition, be specific about your song preferences and the scheduling of the bride and groom's first dance, the bride's dance with her father and the groom's dance with his mother, the toasts, the cutting of the cake, and the last dance before you leave for the honeymoon.

From a musical perspective, think about your wedding reception in two or three segments: first will be when guests mingle over cocktails or hors d'oeuvres (the music should serve as a backdrop for conversation—a string quartet or a jazz trio perhaps); next is the meal, when a variety of tunes that appeal to all the guests is best; dancing typically follows, and here you can have anything from a classic big band sound to karaoke, depending on your wedding theme and what you like to get on down to.

Food and Drink

When deciding on the type of food service that you want to offer your family members and friends, you'll want to take into account the time of day and the venue, along with the style you want for your reception.

What are your options?

A morning affair calls for breakfast or brunch—omelettes or eggs Benedict, waffles or crepes, fresh fruit and pastries. An early day celebration begs for salads and light entrées. Opt for a picnic or barbecue for a more informal daytime meal. Afternoon or evening celebrations are perfect for a cocktail reception, with hot and cold hors d'oeuvres presented as a buffet or passed by waiters. An evening function requires a substantial dinner-like menu, perhaps served in several courses.

Depending on the number of guests you are having, you can decide to do the catering yourself (with a little help!), use the staff available at the venue, or hire an outside caterer. Discuss the kind of menu you want and ask for a few suggestions to choose from. As our bride and groom to be quickly discovered, all caterers should offer tasting sessions—or freebies!—where you can make a final selection from a number of dishes. (Remember to include a vegetarian or ingredient-intolerant option if required.)

Having the caterer or the venue provide the drinks is an easy option, but can often end up being more expensive, particularly if you have an open bar. If you are lucky to live within driving distance of a wholesale supplier or, better still, a vineyard, you can purchase drinks at considerably lower prices.

Go the distance

Instead of the usual wedding fare, look to the world of international cuisine: opt for trays of sushi, satays, and bento boxes; echo your honeymoon theme with Moroccan tagines, Thai curry, and so on; or host the most extravagant picnic ever, with bruschetta, ripe cheeses, and summer fruits.

The wedding cake

This is one of the oldest wedding traditions, and is something else that can reflect your wedding theme. Traditionally, the cake is a tiered, rich, moist cake with icing, but recently there has been a move to vary the style of the cake.

These days, you can opt for whatever shape cake appeals to you—a person, a building, a work of art—and the flavor, filling, and icing can be a combination of anything you like. Some of the most popular pairings are pound cake with butter cream icing, carrot cake with cream cheese icing, and chocolate cake with white chocolate icing. Mmm. . .

Aim to have a pretty good idea of what you want before you start looking for a baker. Gather together pictures from magazines and look on the Internet for ideas, and always be prepared to take advice from the baker as well. If you get really stuck, head to the store that makes the tastiest cakes in town and see if they can offer you direction.

And for dessert?

Don't want cake? Serve a to-die-for dessert instead. . . Take inspiration from the French and have a towering confection of chocolate profiteroles, called a *croquembouche*. Or how about serving individual cupcakes, one for each guest?

Photography

The photographer is probably the single most important professional to take part in a wedding. He or she is charged with capturing all the events of the day and plays a large part in scheduling and organizing the sequence of those events.

For this reason alone you should put your faith in a recommended professional when it comes to preserving the Big Day in pictures. The best are in high demand, so you'll want to book ASAP. Ask for recommendations, make notes of names in wedding magazines, and search the Internet to get a feel for photographers' work. Schedule face-to-face interviews, and ask to see sample albums to get an idea of the photographer's style. Discuss the fee structure, the payment schedule, and when you could expect proofs and the final album.

Once you've found a photographer that shares the same vision as you, provide him or her with all the details, including the schedule, the number and names of the wedding party, and sticky situations that may require special care. Talk about your preference for posed as well as candid shots, a list of must-have shots, e.g., Grandma Mabel, Great-Aunt Bertha, and you, and the layout of the album that will ultimately be created.

Mix it up

You don't have to go for one style of photography over another. Sure, hire the pro to take posed shots after the ceremony—these will likely be the images that stand the test of time. But go for reportage shots, too: have friends circulate a Polaroid camera or place disposable cameras on the tables at the reception. With a mixture of color and black-and-white film, you'll get to remember both the formality and the relaxed ambience of the occasion.

Videos

A video can capture moments that photography can't. Just like searching for your photographer, start to interview videographers early on. Ask to view samples and pay attention to how the videographer moves from scene to scene, whether he or she has a steady hand, and that the imagery is in focus.

Reception etiquette

There are a number of conventions that take place at the reception: a traditional seating plan, speeches, the first dance, and tossing the bouquet are some of them. It is entirely up to you and your fiancé whether they have a part to play on your wedding day.

The pros and cons of a receiving line

You may well balk at the idea of having a receiving line at your wedding, but the purpose is simple: it allows every guest to express his or her best wishes to the newlyweds and congratulations to their parents. It makes sense to stage the receiving line at the entrance to the reception.

As the hostess of the reception, the mother of the bride heads the line. The mother of the groom, and the bride and groom, follow her. The maid of honor and best man may be included at the end of the line if they know a lot of guests. It would be rude for anyone to leave the receiving line before the last guest has had a chance to offer congratulations.

What's the alternative? If you decide against it, you should allow enough time at the beginning of the reception for the newlyweds and their parents to circulate among the guests, making an effort to speak to everyone.

The seating plan

Decisions over your seating plan will be influenced by the layout of the reception site and the number of guests you have invited. Traditionally, the newlyweds sit at the center of a long table that faces the rest of the guests, and they are flanked on either side by the remaining members of the wedding party. Alternatives to this arrangement are for the parents of the bride and groom to be seated together, hosting a table of their own and joined by family and close friends. A recent trend is for the bride and groom to be seated at a small table for two to celebrate their first meal together, surrounded by tables of their wedding party members.

Toasts and speeches

One of the most sentimental and historic of wedding customs is the wedding toast. It's the best man's responsibility to take center stage as soon as guests are comfortably seated at the reception and presented with something to drink, or before the newlyweds cut the cake.

Champagne is a popular choice for toasting. If the crowd is large, use a microphone so that everyone can hear what is said. At the end of his speech, the best man proposes a toast and the guests raise their glasses. The bride and groom should remain seated and smile in appreciation of the good wishes.

The groom should then step forward to thank the best man for his kind words, and offer a toast to his new wife, his new in-laws, and his own parents. The bride can also offer a toast to her new husband and to the parents.

It is up to you whether you follow tradition or not. If the best man is cripplingly shy or your Mom wants to make the big speech, so be it.

> **"My brother and sister-in-law broke all the rules when they got married last year and asked their maid of honor to give the main speech. She was funny yet respectful, emotional but not sentimental. It was the most moving wedding speech I have ever heard."** Kate, 36

The first dance

Whether at the beginning of the reception, or as the music starts after the meal, there will come the time when you both hit the

> **"**I hated every minute of our first dance. It seemed to go on forever and we both felt pretty awkward. It certainly wasn't the romantic schmooze we had both practiced. The bandleader realized, completely changed the tempo, and joined us on the dance floor. He really saved the day!**"**
> Beth, 32

dance floor for your first steps as husband and wife. Your choice of song may be a sentimental classic, or may have been a popular tune when you were dating, but if you're wearing a bulky gown, it should have a slow to medium beat to allow you to dance effortlessly. If neither of you are great dancers, you could take lessons or at least practice beforehand until you can move smoothly together.

Alternatives to this custom are for the bride and groom to take to the floor for the first few minutes of the dance—so that pictures can be taken—and for the rest of the wedding party to join in shortly after. If the idea of the first dance fills you with horror, you can do away with it altogether or make it the "last dance" of the evening before you make your honeymoon exit!

Tossing the bouquet

The gathering of the unmarried, female guests at the reception often signals the beginning of the end of the celebrations, as the bride turns her back to the crowd and pitches the bouquet over her head. For brides choosing to preserve their wedding-day flowers, consider ordering a "toss" bouquet from your florist for this festivity.

The honeymoon getaway

The bride and groom are traditionally the first to leave the reception, applauded by guests tossing confetti or rice, or forming an archway as they depart for their honeymoon. There is nothing to stop couples from staying for the entire duration of the party, but tell guests your plan so that they do not stay longer than they wish to themselves, waiting to send you off formally.

Making a difference

Your wedding will be remembered for the elements that make it personal to you both, and to that end, there are special touches (and outright showstoppers) that you can incorporate in both the marriage service and the celebration that follows.

Special touches

For the service, design a program that identifies members of the wedding party and lists each part of the ceremony. The style of the program should follow the same design theme as your invitations, and can be passed out by the groomsmen or ushers as they seat the guests on arrival.

At the reception, present a small gift at each place setting, ranging from a tiny frame with a photo of the two of you, a CD of your favorite love songs, a bundle of sugared almonds wrapped in tulle, or a packet of flower seeds to commemorate the beginning and growth of your marriage.

Move away from the traditional throwing of rice and confetti and use petals, potpourri, or bubbles.

As you leave the reception, have your guests stand along both sides of the exit path holding burning sparklers for a glistening send-off, or organize a dazzling firework display.

Showstoppers

Venue and budget permitting, here are some ideas if you really want to pull out all the stops:

- Releasing white doves or butterflies at the completion of the ceremony
- Announcing the completion of the ceremony in skywriting
- Hiring a magician and performers to mingle among the crowd as the reception kicks off
- Hiring a celebrity musician for the evening reception
- Renting a snow machine for snowflakes at a winter celebration

Bridal registry

Thanks to the bridal registry services at department and specialty stores, you can have a gift list that is all taken care of in one place.

For couples that have either lived on their own for a while or lived together before the wedding, and who have already accumulated many of the everyday items for their home, the bridal registry may seem less important. However, asking for money is considered poor taste. Instead, have your parents inform inquiring guests that you'd be grateful to receive gifts of vouchers or cash that would be used toward a major purchase or a deposit on a house.

Want to be less conventional?

If you already have the domestic baggage to last a lifetime (and are happy with it), here are a few ideas for an alternative wish list:

- Charitable donations
- Tickets to a sporting event, the theater, an exhibition, or a gig
- Gift certificates for your favorite store, restaurant, theme park, or garden nursery
- A case of wine, champagne, or virgin olive oil
- Contributions to your music, cacti, or vodka collection
- Luxury goodies for the honeymoon trip

> **"**We found an easy solution to our gift list and decided to replace older gadgets with new, improved ones. A few weeks before the wedding, we picked out our stuff and went to a rummage sale. This way we were able to pocket extra cash for the honeymoon and redecorate our home with brand-new gifts at the same time.**"** Jackie, 37

Survival tactics

You are going to be hiring a good number of professionals over the next few months—a photographer, a florist, a baker, a stationer, musicians, caterers, and more. Simply coordinating them will be a task in itself and there are ways of making your life easier.

Always do your homework. Look through magazines, surf the Internet, and ask friends and family for recommendations. Before even picking up the phone, have a very clear idea of the look, sound, and flavor of whatever it is you are asking for.

Ask to see examples of previous work, certificates or proof of qualifications, commendations from happy customers, newspaper or magazine articles—anything that confirms you are getting the level of expertise you want.

Keep a close eye on your budget and stick to it. Be up front with all professionals from the very beginning. Do not be persuaded to increase your budget unless it is for something simply amazing.

Agree to a realistic time frame. Check out other commitments your suppliers may have and make sure they are not going to interfere with yours.

Get everything in writing, confirming who is to do what, by when, and include a payment schedule.

Resources

Wedding planning

The Association of Bridal Consultants
Tel: 860/355-0464
www.bridalassn.com

Association of Certified Professional
Wedding Consultants
Tel: 408/528-9000
www.acpwc.com

www.bridalguide.com

www.brides.com

www.weddingplanningwiz.com

Wedding photography

Professional Photographers of America
Tel: 800/786-6277
www.ppa.com

Wedding & Event Videographers Association
International
Tel: 941/923-5334
www.weva.com

Catering

International Caterers Association
Tel: 888/604-5844
www.icacater.org

Wedding flowers

Floralshops.com
www.floralshops.com

Reception music

National Association of Mobile Entertainers
www.djkj.com

www.gigmasters.com

Wedding programs

www.theamericanwedding.com

www.myweddinginvitations.com

Bridal registry

www.aperfectweddinggift.com

www.thebigday.com

www.weddingchannel.com

Wedding showstoppers

www.fireworksexpress.com

www.usairads.com

Chapter Five

What To Wear (And How)

So the venue's chosen, the invitations are being written, and your theme is finally decided. All you need to think about now is what you are going to wear on the most important day of your life. This is where some brides are more fortunate than others, having spent their teenage years designing wedding dresses in their school notebooks. If you weren't one of those girls—or even if you were—you're going to need to source a dress, shoes, and hairstyle to inspire admiration, and perhaps a little envy, in everyone.

The dress

Surfed Internet today in search of second-hand wedding dress. Had to really—our budget is blown and there's no way I can afford a new one. Can't believe how expensive they are. Even the most hideous off-the-rack dresses are about $2,000. Am I missing something? You do just wear it for one day, right?

Not that going to the shops was all bad; assistants are great, everyone is very happy, and you get free coffee. Even someone else's Mom got teary when I emerged in one dress. (Not that mine did. She was at home watching daytime TV—said I was hell to shop with.) Might have helped if someone had warned me to wear my best underwear, though. I was in gray, holey panties, and no bra (blush). Assistants were in and out of the dressing room like crazy people. "How are you getting along?" they'd shout seconds after giving me a dress to put on, tearing the curtain wide open for everyone to see.

So, the Internet. Found an incredible site where real-life brides post photos of their wedding alongside an ad for the dress. So funny. Too funny, in cruel way. The photos were hilarious (where did they find those grooms? Ick!), but the best parts were their comments. "Everyone said I looked beautiful in my dress," wrote one. They lied.

Got very organized in the afternoon and bought a wedding magazine for ideas. So hard to choose. Maybe if I'd been more romantic as a teenager I'd have planned everything long ago. I wasn't. Never thought I would ever get long-term boyfriend, let alone husband. So now feel woefully unprepared. And all bridal models seem stick-thin. Of course they'd look good in tight, shiny, white satin, but can't help thinking I'd look like a blimp. But in back of magazine was ad for local woman who sells second-hand dresses.

Paid a visit after work. Unbelievable! Room full of dresses all hung up over walls. Racks and racks. Everything. And all worn just the once, so perfect condition. (Can't help thinking mine won't be though, bound to be covered in wine, grass stains, tears, and worse—and that's just on way to service.) Tried on loads, until . . .

I FOUND THE DRESS. It is so perfect. Ivory duchess satin (whatever that means), full-length in two pieces. Corset top, with ties around back and chiffon sleeves. (Essential since when naked, my arms look like bat wings.) Skirt is full length, sort of A-line, with petticoats. Heaven! Made woman tie ribbons so tight almost fainted. But boobs look great. Satin so smooth that I have two boobs visible, instead of the one long bolster I had in other dresses.

Even the woman said it suited me. (And she wasn't a woman given to meaningless praise.) In fact, she had already told me that I should "do something about that hair" and "lose a few pounds before the Big Day." What was with her? So different to fawning assistants in bridal shops. Was she bitter, jilted woman committed to heaping misery on young brides? Or am I just fat cow with bad hair? Hmm.

Despite her weight comment, it fits perfectly. And is half its original (designer's naturally) price. And is so gorgeous, I won't need any jewelry. All need to get is shoes. I'm thinking crushed velvet, dark blue, with pointy toe. Gothic-style. And brides-maids can wear dark-blue dresses. (Really wish had guts to put them into fuschia crinoline ra-ra dresses, like threaten to when drunk.)

But my dress. It's soooo perfect. My only fear is superstition—what if woman who wore it first time is divorced already? (Dress is year old, apparently.) What if dress is made from unlucky, cursed satin, woven by jilted witch? What if whoever wears it is doomed to die alone?

Dress is so sexy, even if J. doesn't show up, someone else'll marry me. I do look very good in it. Who'd have thought? Shall have to get married lots of times.

What's your style?

Many brides start off determined to wear anything but white on the Big Day, yet find themselves drawn in that direction once they start looking.

The outfit you choose may well depend on the size and style of the occasion. The more formal the wedding, the closer you will get to the full-length, full-blown gown. But don't be put off wearing a dress altogether if a traditional look is not your style. First off, the dress does not have to be white (or any shade of cream through ivory for that matter). There are pastel options ranging from subtle blues and pinks to cappuccino brown, lilac, and pistachio. For a richer, more luxuriant look, consider emerald, scarlet, or burgundy velvet. Brides looking for the ultimate fairy-tale look can go for metallics, starting with gold and silver, but also shimmery blues and pinks.

There is also hope for brides who hesitate at the idea of swathes of satin, embroidered bodices, and trailing trains, since your choice of dress style is inexhaustible—particularly if you do see yourself wearing white. A wedding dress does not have to be complicated in design, neither does it have to be full length. Depending on your size and shape (see pages 68-69) you can opt for soft flowing lines or something skimpy, fresh, and fun. Consider wearing a suit and not a dress, and you get to mix and match style and color, too. Instead of heavy brocade, have fun with beads, sequins, sew-on butterflies, or flowers.

If you are still unsure, why not look to your wedding theme for inspiration (see pages 23-25). A hot summer wedding might call for a simple-cut floral dress in a country setting, a batik-style mini-sundress for an on-the-beach affair, or a stylish suit for a ceremony on board a cruise ship or yacht. The colder months suggest soft, warm velvets, vintage for a Victorian theme, and earthy tones for a fall wedding.

"I knew from the start that I wanted to wear deep red satin. We kept it a secret from my fiancé and now, five years on, Peter still insists that the highlight of his day was seeing me for the first time." Lucy, 37

The bridesmaids' attire

There's an age-old joke about all the expensive but hideous bridesmaids' dresses that one can accumulate as your friends lose their otherwise impeccable fashion sense and succumb to bridal mania.

Though true in some cases (a bridesmaid can console herself in vain that there WILL BE another occasion, someday, possibly even a Halloween party where she can wear the dress), it doesn't have to be this way. While there is a tradition for all bridesmaids to wear the same style dress, regardless of size or skin tone, it is no longer practiced at all weddings, and there are a number of alternatives available to the modern bride.

What are your options?

If you have bridesmaids of a similar size and shape, you can certainly opt for the same style dress, but have each maid in a different color or tone to complement your own. However, after determining some basic parameters, like length and formality, you might choose a theme color and have each attendant find a dress style in that color that she really likes and that suits her.

If you are having the dresses made, you'll want to start shopping at least six months in advance to allow plenty of time for delivery and any alterations that might need to be made. Alterations are typically included in the prices offered at full-service boutiques, except in the case of sale dresses, where there is an added charge.

Customarily, the bridesmaids pay for their own dresses plus matching shoes. This can amount to a considerable expense—even more so once accessories have been added to the shopping list—and you would do well to bear this in mind when deciding on a style for your bridesmaids. In cases where the shoes won't show under a floor-length gown, the bride may choose a basic style of shoe she prefers and let each maid make her own purchase, accepting they will not all be exactly the same in design.

Matching jewelry, given as a gift by the bride, accentuates the gown and lowers the costs for each of her bridesmaids. For a traditional look, bridesmaids should wear the same jewelry, but none should wear a watch on the day.

What shape are you?

Before doing anything, be completely honest with yourself and the mirror in recognizing your best and worst features. You'll want a dress that accentuates your good parts, but minimizes the parts you are not so happy with.

Short

Good: gowns that have vertical lines or decoration to give the illusion of height.
Not so good: heavy fabrics and complex ornamentation.

Tall

Good: gowns with sophisticated and sweeping lines; satin and linen fabrics.
Not so good: gowns with vertical lines or decoration.

Large bust

Good: an off-the-shoulder dress or one with an open, shaped neckline; a fitted waistline or low-cut back to draw the eye away from the bosom.
Not so good: a high neckline; a high waistline; elaborate detailing on the bodice.

Small bust

Good: loose, fitted bodice with high neck and covered shoulders; deep V- or scoop back; full, embellished skirt.
Not so good: a tight bodice or open neckline; any necklace.

Shapely legs

Good: short, above-the-knee skirt; sheath with side split.
Not so good: billowing, ball-gown skirt.

Dark-skinned

Good: white fabrics or pale pastel tones.
Not so good: ivory colorations with yellow undertones.

Fair-skinned

Good: warm naturals and various ivory colors.

Not so good: stark white, which tends to wash out pale tones.

Small waist

Good: gowns with fitted waists and decorated bodices; off-the-shoulder necklines and gathered skirts.

Not so good: decoration on both bodice and skirt.

Full figure

Good: lightweight, matte fabrics; V-, keyhole,- or scoop-necklines; empire waists and A-line shapes.

Not so good: bulky or glossy fabrics; puffed or full sleeves; large back bow; pouf veil.

Unshapely arms

Good: sleeves; a shaped neckline; a decorative bodice.

Not so good: sleeveless, off-the-shoulder, or halter styles.

Thick waist

Good: an off-the-shoulder design or one with an empire waist; a deep or open neckline to call attention upward; an elongated waistline and fancy skirt to call attention downward.

Not so good: any detail at the waist or a heavily embellished bodice.

Pear-shaped

Good: a gentle princess line will create a slimming effect; a decorative bodice with a scoop- or V-neck to draw attention upward.

Not so good: any detail at the waist; a full, embellished skirt; any decorative trimming along the hemline.

Buying your gown

You'll probably put a day aside for visiting bridal boutiques or your favorite department stores to find something you like and can afford. Don't be surprised if that day turns into many days before the perfect dress is found!

With this in mind it makes sense to get started on the hunt for your dress as soon as you have decided on the type of wedding you both want. A four- to six-month lead time is advised for ordering a dress and having it custom fitted before the Big Day.

Know what you want

Get some ideas before you shop—a good place to start is by looking at every bridal magazine you can get your hands on! Photographs of gowns dominate the pages, and you'll soon be able to spot the latest trends. Pick out the styles that you like, and take pictures with you. Maybe you are wild about just one detail rather than the entire style of a dress—take that with you, too.

Make an appointment at a full-service boutique, where you can enlist the aid of an experienced bridal consultant who has assisted numerous brides before you. Describe the wedding that you are planning, and let her know the budget you are working with for your gown and accessories. Show her photos of gowns that you admire, and ask her to show you examples that she thinks will meet all of your criteria. You will be trying dresses on, so learn from our bride to be's mistakes and wear appropriate underwear, and arrange your hair similarly to the way you plan to wear it on your wedding day (see page 74).

Make an appointment for a first fitting as soon as you have chosen your dress, and an appointment for a final fitting two weeks before the wedding for any last-minute changes.

You should be prepared to place a 50 percent deposit when you order your dress, with the balance due when you pick it up before the wedding.

Bride on a budget

Not every bride will consider her gown to be the most important facet of the wedding, and would prefer to see the money going elsewhere. Luckily, there are lots of options for every style and bank balance.

Your first stop might be a consignment shop that carries once-worn bridal gowns. Take note that while you may be able to buy the dress very inexpensively, you will still have to find a talented dressmaker who can fit the dress perfectly to your figure. If you know someone who is a dressmaker, you could have your dream dress for an affordable fee.

Look out for bridal salon sales of sample dresses or discontinued styles. The boutique might also provide the alterations and professional cleaning of a sale dress for an additional charge.

Your perfect dress might not be new or even nearly-new—how about wearing a vintage gown or a family heirloom? You may still need to pay for alterations and cleaning to get it in perfect shape for your big day, though.

Preserving your gown

The job of preserving a wedding gown should be entrusted only to a professional. Although your favorite dry cleaner has performed miracles on many of your outfits in the past, the task is best directed to a specialist who is trained in treating highly delicate fabrics with embellished details.

To the naked eye, your dress may appear to be in great shape, but in reality, it's been soiled by perspiration, champagne, wine, and countless other substances that will, untreated, break down the fabric and stain it. You need a professional who can deal with the soiling without damaging the materials.

At the same time, if you plan on keeping your dress, you'll want to have the gown wrapped in acid-free paper and packed for storage in an acid-free box. Avoid an airtight container, as mold may develop, or a transparent box, since the biggest enemy to your dress is light. Once complete, store the box at a moderate temperature where it won't be subject to either overheating or extreme cold.

Finishing touches

You will be the center of attention for the whole day. While your dress will certainly be the main focus, it is the accessories that will be working together to complete the look successfully.

Headpieces

Any headpiece should flatter the shape of your face and blend with your hairstyle. It may be made of the same fabric as your gown, made of a similar material, or be designed around a tiara. Most bridal gowns take on a classier look with the addition of a veil, which can range in length from elbow-length to the longest 20-foot cathedral veil. Often, a headpiece is constructed with a removable veil that allows you to move freely after the service. For a less traditional look, opt for a hat or wear flowers in your hair.

Jewelry

The fabric and decorative detail of your gown will dictate the type of jewelry you wear. Pearls have been the classic gem in bridal jewelry for years, and are now being updated with sparkling rhinestones.

Dresses with an open neckline beg for either a necklace with tiny earrings, or just some elaborate, dangling earrings. Sleeveless or short-sleeve styles may be enhanced with a bracelet. But if your gown has a high neck and long sleeves, the only extra jewelry you'll want will be some delicate earrings.

Lingerie

Under your gown, you'll need the very best foundations to help your dress sit smoothly and comfortably. A full skirt will need some kind of underskirt for support, and this can be attached to the inside of the gown or worn as an independent item. For bridal hosiery, you can choose anything from fine silk stockings to lacy knit tights and those with patterned motifs. Most of these will be available in varying shades to match your dress or outfit.

Shoes

As you shop for shoes, remember that you will spend most of your wedding day on your feet, so you'll want an extremely comfortable fit. Hours of standing and dancing will influence you in choosing a comfortable heel. Another important consideration is your height next to your groom.

If finding a pair of shoes to match the color of your outfit proves difficult, some bridal stores will dye shoes for you at an additional cost.

Handbag

Although a handbag doesn't often come to mind when thinking about wedding accessories, every bride will want somewhere to put her lipstick, perfume, and a tissue or handkerchief. Select a tiny purse, and assign your maid of honor the task of holding on to it for you.

Seasonal considerations

Depending on the time of year, there are a couple of extras to think about: during cooler months, you'll want a wrap to keep you warm as you enter and exit the ceremony and reception; if there is the possibility of rainy weather, you may want to shop for an umbrella that's large enough to protect you and your dress; or, perhaps it will be hot, so it might be worth investing in a pretty parasol to provide shade, and a tube of sunscreen.

Wedding day beauty

Every bride will want to feel beautiful on her wedding day and it pays to spend time on achieving this. Natural beauty is the starting point for any good look, so play up your assets!

Your hair

Consider your options early on so that you can try out styles in the months before the wedding. Do you have a short, face-framing cut that you want to let grow out a little? Or, if your hair is long, do you want to wear it up or down?

Talk to your stylist about your dress and headpiece so he or she can assess how best to arrange your hair. More importantly, let him or her determine how to attach the headpiece comfortably so that it stays put on the day.

Make an appointment with your hairdresser to have your hair trimmed and/or color-treated two to three weeks before the wedding, and a second appointment for styling on the day of the wedding. If you are planning something elaborate, it is essential to make a separate appointment so your stylist can have a trial run.

Your makeup

Depending on how skilled you are at applying makeup, you might be able to do it yourself based on a consultation with a consultant at your favorite department or specialty store. Tell her about the time and place of your wedding, and describe your gown and headpiece, as well as your jewelry. She'll be able to enhance your current makeup application with new shades that are appropriate for the lighting at your wedding. Give yourself plenty of time to practice applying the products.

If you're not particularly expert in putting on makeup, you may want to hire a makeup artist to be sure that your look is perfect from beginning to end. Arrange a trial run a few weeks before the wedding and decide on the look that suits you the best. Have the stylist come to your home on the morning of the wedding, at least two hours before you are scheduled to leave.

A natural look

An attractive look for a bride on her wedding day is a warm, natural one. Use makeup effectively to look your best.

Start with a soft foundation that isn't too white (it can make you appear washed out in the photographs), but which is consistent with the skin tone of your neck and arms. Complete this first step with finishing powder, applied with a big fan brush.

Even the most well-rested bride will need some under-eye concealer to hide darker tones. Rather than applying a white concealer, place a dab of light concealer in the inner corner of the eye near the bridge and a slightly deeper shade for the outer part of the under eye. Next, choose a shadow in a natural shade, along with liner to define the shape of your eyes, and finish with mascara. Essential in bringing attention to the eyes is the proper application of blush, which should only be placed on the cheek to temple area.

Your body

Staying in shape by exercising and eating well will not only help you look gorgeous on the day, but will also offer respite from all the planning and the occasional tensions that crop up. If you are hoping to lose weight, though—and there is no rule that says you have to—remember that any change in weight will affect the fit of your outfit.

Shape up

You can immediately look and feel better by adding some physical activity to your daily agenda, and by adopting healthy eating habits. For the maximum benefit, start a new exercise and diet plan early and not just a couple of weeks before the wedding. You shouldn't be starving yourself at the last minute in an attempt to drop a few pounds for the Big Day, especially when you will be tired from juggling the final details.

Don't overdo it in the beginning or you may burn out. Set up an exercise schedule that fits into your busy lifestyle. Talk to your physician or personal trainer to determine what types of exercise would be most beneficial to you and the easiest to fit into your allotted time. In fact, a visit with your doctor is a great way to start your new routine. Check your weight and blood pressure and have a cholesterol screening. Talk to your doctor about your goals, and ask for a daily calorie count that is appropriate for your height, weight, and age.

You'll need a minimum of at least 20 minutes of aerobic activity four to six times a week. Walking, cycling, and swimming are activities that you can do alone, and are convenient to fit into any schedule. If you don't have the discipline for exercising alone, a group sport like tennis, squash, or soccer might be a better option. Maybe you and your fiancé can even find something that you can do together, which may well be a welcome break from what can easily become constant talk of wedding preparations.

To get the maximum benefit from your exercise program, integrate some weight training to tone and shape your muscles. Try both free weights and exercise machines to determine which feels more comfortable to you. In combination with aerobics, weight training helps to build muscle and activates your metabolism. Muscles use up more energy and take up less space than fat. Just a few weeks of regular exercise can make noticeable improvements to the definition of your arms and legs. (Take note that a bride to be who diets without exercise will lose muscle tone as well as fat.)

Finally, aim to take in eight to ten glasses of water each day (at least 3 pints or 1.5 liters). This is even more important if you are exercising regularly. If your body tends to retain water, cut back on your sodium intake, which will reduce water retention.

Be sure to let your body rest one day per week and make sure that you are getting plenty of sleep each night, and taking the opportunity to relax on the weekends. You should expect to feel a little tired during the first couple of weeks in a new exercise program, but don't push yourself so hard that you are constantly exhausted.

What are you eating?

Never drastically cut back on your food intake hoping to lose weight that way, since your body will rebel and leave you worn down, irritable, and exhausted. Start the day with breakfast: this will jump-start your metabolism, replenish the body's low blood sugar levels, and provide you with the energy you need. And even if you are determined to drop a few pounds before the wedding day, don't deprive yourself of an occasional treat; just try to make it a healthy one.

Survival tactics

On a personal level, you will want to look great and feel great on your wedding day. If you are not sure of the impression you want to give, look through a couple of magazines for inspiration, but don't make the mistake of thinking that everything you see will be right for you.

Get it right from the start

It is generally a bad idea to go for a completely new look. Concentrate instead on looking the best version of YOU, and not someone your guests or groom will barely recognize.

Take a friend

When it comes to buying a gown, sales assistants and consultants will offer you all the professional advice you need, but don't think it stops there. Take a close friend with you when you shop—someone who knows you well and who can be relied on to be truthful. Picking the right person could be one of the most significant decisions of your entire planning strategy.

Avoid typical mistakes

Whatever you do, don't try anything permanent (like a new hair color or extensions) the week before your wedding.

Emergency diet aids

If you are finding it impossible to stick to your diet, check out your local salon to see if it offers body-wrap treatments. While you are at it, investigate the life-saving world of miracle underwear for a flatter tummy, tighter behind, and thinner thighs.

Resources

Choosing your gown

101 Bridal Gowns
Tel: 800/950-8238
www.101bridalgowns.com

Bridal Guide
Tel: 800/472-7744
www.bridalguide.com

The Knot.com
Tel: 877/843-5668
www.theknot.com

TodaysBride.com
Tel: 877/417-7419
www.todaysbride.com

A Vintage Wedding
Tel: 800/660-3640
www.vintagewedding.com

Wedding Gazette
Tel: 617/275-7270
www.weddinggazette.com

Wedding Solutions
Tel: 800/606-9200
www.weddingsolutions.com

www.banquethall.com

California Bridal Guide
Tel: 877/645-8885
www.californiabridalguide.com

www.perfectweddingguide.com

www.thewedguide.com

www.todays-weddings.com

www.usabride.com

www.weddingchannel.com

www.weddinggownspecialists.com

On a budget

www.bridepower.com

www.yesteryearbridals.com

Consignment wedding gowns

Cherished
Tel: 925/280-0128
www.cherishedweddinggowns.com

Usedweddingdresses.com
Tel: 972/365-7603
www.usedweddingdresses.com

Chapter Six

The Groom's Guide

While you are busy sorting out roses and raffia, or focusing on how to wear your hair, your fiancé should be making a few plans of his own. Once the two of you have decided on your honeymoon destination, he can make the travel arrangements. And of course he will need to organize the men's formalwear. The groom can also help by working out how to get everyone from A to B on the Big Day. And he'll have his best man to come to his aid if necessary!

Hopes about the honeymoon

Have been reading a lot of celebrity-gossip magazines to get ideas about honeymoons. Wish hadn't. Am sickened that some of them get to enjoy three months in Paris/Rome/Rio, whereas J. and I will get ten days . . . Where?

And there's the question. J. is determined to arrange all honeymoon himself. Bless. He is getting more and more manly as months go by. He has even become suspiciously mysterious about the wedding night. We don't want to stay at same place as the wedding, since guests all staying there and we don't want to face them all the next day. (Is that odd?) Waving to our parents over breakfast—no, thanks. So J. has arranged something. Or is planning to. Suppose not vitally important—it's not as if that night will be THE night. The FIRST night. It'll probably be the 6,000th. Probably be too tired for sex. (Although, I don't know . . .)

I jokingly asked J. to work out the honeymoon, but never thought he'd take it that seriously. This is good, though, as have realized that I'm happy to let him get involved and help. I trust his taste, he knows mine, and I know that he'll make great choices. That's good, isn't it? With some ex-boyfriends, I wouldn't have trusted them to book me a long weekend. But I know J.'ll do us right.

Have had unexpected bonus too: J.'s parents have said they'll give us $15,000 as a wedding present. Cha-ching! Obviously, in a sensible world this would be put toward curtains for new house and/or savings account. But, in our world, the real, penniless world, a lot will go toward honeymoon.

J. has asked me where I'd like to go, as in overseas or home. Visions of Paris/Rome/Rio flashed before my eyes for a brief second, then disappeared—to be replaced by . . . Hawaii. Yup. I really want to go to Hawaii—partly because I just discovered that both our parents went there on their honeymoons. Since they're all still married today, can't help feeling it's lucky. And we get so much more for our money if we don't have to spend such a huge chunk on airfares.

That's all I've been allowed to say, though. He really does want to do it all himself. So he's spending hours on Internet every evening, choosing.

What I'd ideally love is a hotel on Maui. Want to be pampered. Want hotel room service and mini bar. In my vision, we wake up amid rumpled white sheets and look across room to French windows opening out to a beach. There's a knock on the door—breakfast, with snowy napkins and a single red rose. We get up three hours later, stroll to a restaurant for lunch, then go walking on the beach. Back to hotel, get sexy, have a bath and beautify, then eat dinner on the candlelit verandah, gazing into each other's eyes and telling each other . . .

J. hasn't really said what he'd like. For once, he's being unopinionated. He's just asking me lots of questions, and then becoming all unreadable. Very sexy.

Have no idea what it'll really be like—J. and I have never been on vacation together. Can't picture him as vacation companion. Will he be lazy tourist or guide-book wielding explorer? Hope not latter. Exhausting. And I've bought a lot of high-heels to wear on honeymoon.

It'll just be nice to be together, after all fuss of planning wedding. Just him and me, with time to remember everything about the day, and plan our future together. Holding hands and gathering seashells . . .

Oooh! So excited. Really want to call him and discuss, but—guess what? Busy. (Like me!) He's on the Internet again.

Back to celeb mags for me. It's all consuming, this researching.

The basics

Today's grooms are more involved than ever in planning for their special day. There are plenty of tasks that you as a couple can share, but there are also details that your fiancé can complete alone, or at least with the help of his best man.

While some men want to take part in visiting venues and interviewing wedding professionals, helping with the photography, the music, or the food, others are less interested in the detail. You should assess your fiancé's level of interest, act accordingly, and keep him informed as major arrangements fall into place. However:

- It's the groom who selects the formalwear shop and chooses the styles for the men of the wedding party and the fathers. What he wears at the altar is determined by the time and formality of the wedding celebration (see page 92).

- Most men take little interest in the bride's or bridesmaids' finery, but the groom should be consulted on the design of the boutonnieres.

- One job that he must start on early is the plan for the wedding night.

- He'll also need to supply addresses for his friends on the invitations list, as well as pitch in writing thank-you notes for gifts from his family and friends.

- He will coordinate the transportation details on the wedding day, culminating with the honeymoon getaway.

- The groom should play an active role in helping to coordinate the attendants at the rehearsal so that he knows what will take place at each point in the ceremony.

- As the wedding day draws closer, he'll need to help with the legal paperwork, choose gifts for his attendants, and pick up the wedding rings from the jeweler.

- Of course he also needs to take time for his bride throughout the engagement, and try to keep stress to a minimum!

The grand finale

Tradition has the groom taking responsibility for picking the honeymoon destination and making the travel arrangements as a surprise to his new wife, but
things have changed, and engaged couples today usually make the honeymoon
arrangements together.

Once you have an idea of the kind of trip you think you want, it's time to
start researching the possibilities. Surf the Internet for images of destinations
and attractions, send for information packs from the tourist boards of your
favorite vacation spots, and consult with a professional travel agent.
Determine what your options are, your budget, the time of year you are traveling, and how long you plan to be away.

Do you both enjoy fabulous cuisine and fine dining? Satisfy your cravings
with a trip to wine country in the Loire Valley or the Tuscan Hills.

Are you dreaming of a truly exotic vacation that takes you on an African
safari, a trip to the Far East, or harbors in the seaports of the Mediterranean?
Sign up for a tour, where you really can find the opportunity to be alone as a
couple while taking advantage of an experienced guide.

Do you want the adventure of sailing your own boat, snorkeling through
spectacular reefs, camping on a mountainside, or bicycling from one B&B to
the next? Do you want to learn how to surf or scuba dive? Investigate the
options for a honeymoon that centers on a sport you both enjoy doing
already, or one that you would like to learn.

Or would you prefer to sleep on the beach for the week, soaking up the
sun, sipping fruity cocktails, and flicking through the pages of glossy magazines?

Hotels and resorts make a business of catering to honeymooners, often with
special packages that include unique treats and upgrades. Let the concierge know
in advance and you can probably enjoy a few extra perks. Timeshares are another option, with the possibility of trading reservations for anywhere in the world.

Honeymoon travel tips

Don't skimp on the planning for your honeymoon. The last thing you want after the wedding of your dreams is a honeymoon you won't be able to forget for all the wrong reasons. Here are some tips for traveling with ease and not forgetting any of the specifics.

- Collect as much material as you can on your chosen destination so that you can take advantage of everything available to you both. Guide books will provide basic information, while travel magazines offer more up-to-date activities. Tourist boards will send brochures with points of interest and calendars of special events.

- Plan to interview more than one travel agent to find a professional who is really familiar with where you're traveling and can provide expert advice. Some travel agents belong to large corporations that can offer reduced rates on holiday packages. Others may work for independent businesses or for themselves and have certain specialties like adventure tours or exotic getaways.

- Knowing that all travel agents are not alike, ask for recommendations from friends who share your tastes in traveling. Book an appointment rather than showing up unexpectedly, and carry a list of questions to discuss during your visit. Double-check the quoted rates with airline and hotel websites, and ask about travel insurance.

- Obtain a list of official requirements, and make sure that your personal identification is current. Check your passport and any necessary visas. Inquire about the need for inoculations, and schedule the treatments with your physician in plenty of time before your departure.

- Before you book your reservations, coordinate your work schedules to determine how much vacation time you can use, and whether you want to add a day or so afterward to unpack and settle down into married life.

- If your leave time is limited, plan a short escape and make plans for a later, longer holiday to your real dream destination when the timing is better. Remember that any private time you have together immediately following the wedding will still be special; an intimate weekend in the country will be just as memorable as two weeks on the ski slopes.

Give some thought as to how you'll get to the departure point and, later, home when you return. Arranging transportation for the newly-weds is one of the duties of the best man, but anyone can take over. You'll want to have your bags packed and ready to go before you head out for the marriage ceremony.

Make arrangements for your mail to be handled while you are away. Be sure to leave all your gifts in a safe place, or consider asking a friend to stay at your house in your absence.

Make copies of your marriage certificate and take one with you. If you have changed your name but have not yet changed your identification documents, travel under your maiden name.

As far as reservations are concerned, you will find it easier to travel under your maiden name until all your documentation reflects your new name. This is especially important in this time of heightened security.

Pack romantic extras, such as favorite CDs, massage oils, and lotions. Of course, don't forget your best lingerie!

Choosing the best man

In the same way that a bride may struggle to choose her maid of honor, a groom often wrestles with the decision about whom he'll ask to serve as best man. The selection of the groom's right-hand man is important for both the symbolism of his role and the duties he'll carry out.

Most often, the best man is the groom's closest brother or cousin, or best friend from school or college. In some cultures, it is traditional for the groom's father to take this honor.

While the best man will receive a list of tasks to fulfill, his main contribution is to support the groom in the decisions he makes, and to be a judge of good taste when it comes to making his speech and arranging the bachelor party. He needs to be a conscientious listener, to advise the groom throughout the engagement, and to take part in selecting the appropriate formalwear for all the men in the wedding party. His objective is to make the most special day of the groom's life a success.

The relationship between the groom and his best man may well go back further than that of the groom and his bride, and will continue long after the wedding.

The best man's duties

The best man plays an essential role throughout the engagement and on the wedding day itself, which is focused primarily on activities behind the scenes.

His first active role is typically to assist the groom in picking out the formalwear for the men in the wedding party. In opting for one style over another and offering recommendations for coordinating accessories, he needs to represent the views of the groomsmen, as well as any considerations regarding the bride's outfit.

The best man arranges the bachelor party. Traditionally, this is a night of bar-hopping, but more and more commonly nowadays the best man will arrange and host a guys' weekend away or attendance at a sporting event.

The best man attends the wedding rehearsal in order to learn how the ceremony will proceed the next day. It's his job to corral the other groomsmen and to make sure they all know what they are doing and when.

On the wedding day, his most important task is to make sure that the groom arrives at the ceremony on time and fully dressed with all the items of his outfit. The best man carries the wedding rings to the service, and presents them to the celebrant at the appropriate moment.

Depending on the type of ceremony, the best man will be responsible for delivering the celebrant's payment at a discreet moment.

At the reception, it's the best man who offers the first toast to the newly-weds. After making his speech, he may read out telegrams or emails from absent friends, and then passes on to other guests who want to say a few words.

He makes sure that the bridesmaids have a fleet of dance partners, and double-checks that transportation for the couple's honeymoon getaway is ready on time.

After the wedding he is often involved in dropping off honeymoon luggage to the hotel the newlyweds are staying in, as well as collecting any rented formalwear for cleaning and return.

"Being the best man is not a job to take lightly. I was so honored when Craig asked me to do it that I didn't hesitate to say yes. But I hadn't planned for the overwhelming sense of duty, as well as the fear that if something goes wrong, you are letting a real friend down on the biggest day of his life." **Alex, 26**

The bachelor party

Admittedly, the bride is the one who is bound to get the majority of attention during the engagement. But when it comes to the bachelor party, it's time for a guys' night out and all eyes are on the groom.

A best man will typically want to arrange a memorable event for the groom, and one that allows all of the groom's other close friends and family members to demonstrate their support and friendship.

If friends are widely scattered geographically, the bachelor party needs to be planned with plenty of advance notice to make time for any long-distance travel.

The reputation of the bachelor party has suffered, provoking most of us to conjure up images of raucous behavior, heavy drinking, and hazardous pranks that the groom needs weeks to recover from, not to mention causing late arrivals on the Big Day. However, it is more usual for a group of men to want to spend some time together at a fun venue, taking a trip down memory lane and talking of recent adventures.

Often the venue is driven by a sports outing, such as a round of golf or tickets to a baseball game. The event may be followed by a meal at a favorite restaurant or a night of clubbing.

Ideally, the bachelor party should be scheduled way in advance of the wedding, so that there's ample time for any recovery period. Sometimes, the bachelor and bachelorette parties are hosted simultaneously so the two groups can meet up at a later hour and continue their celebrations together.

Surprise!

An element of the unexpected goes with the territory for a bachelor party and a groom will need to trust his friends to know what he might or might not enjoy.

Formalwear

When it comes to choosing wedding day attire, the men of the bridal party have a much easier time of it than the women. The appropriate clothes are simply determined by tradition, according to the formality and time of day of the celebration. However, make sure you consult with your bride to be when choosing your attire, since you will want to make sure that your attire complements her wedding gown.

Of course all eyes will be on your beautiful bride on the Big Day, but that doesn't mean you shouldn't also set yourself apart. Although it's usually the case that the groom and his henchmen all wear the same or similar outfits, it's essential that your attire on the day sets you apart so that everyone knows you're the guy who gets to kiss the girl at the altar.

What are your options?

- The most common, and classic, jacket style is the tuxedo, and it is usually worn at formal and semi-formal weddings. There are several different choices when it comes to single-breasted or double-breasted, as well as several lapel styles.

- For ultra-formal evening weddings, tails or a tailcoat is called for. This style is cropped in front, with two tails in the back.

- A Mandarin jacket has a stand-up collar and no lapel and is worn with a Mandarin-collared shirt. This combination provides a sneaky way to avoid wearing a tie.

- For a tropical destination wedding, or any celebration taking place in hot weather, a white tuxedo or jacket with black trousers is proper and more comfortable.

- And for the most informal situations, the groom can choose a dark wool suit for fall and winter, or a lighter linen suit for the spring or summer. Another fashionable choice for summer is navy blazer pairred with striped or khaki trousers, complete with a straw hat.

Survival tactics

Not all grooms will find it easy to settle into the role of organizer when it comes to planning his part of the celebrations, and may well have similar anxieties to the bride when it comes to arrangements for the bachelor party and being in the limelight on the Big Day.

The right best man

Most grooms will know who they want to be their best man. If you are struggling over one or two, however, there are several pointers that could help you make a final decision. Firstly, how good are his organizational skills? Secondly, can he be trusted not to embarrass you in his wedding day speech or at the bachelor party?

Bachelor party fears

Don't be fooled into thinking your bachelor party has to be a secret unless you trust your best man implicitly. He should know you well enough to be able to assess what kind of event you would or would not enjoy, but it does not follow that he will be able to resist the temptation to organize some kind of surprise.

The dreaded speeches

Do not leave writing the speech until the last minute; write down ideas as they come to you throughout the engagement and plan to give them form at least a month before the celebration. You cannot rely on spontaneity to carry you through.

Limit all speeches to a maximum of ten minutes.

Keep all speeches clean and avoid referring to issues that will cause embarrassment to other members of the wedding party.

Do not be afraid to practice your speech in front of the mirror in the days before the wedding; the better you know it, the easier it will be to deliver.

Resources

Travel planning

The Knot.com
Tel: 877/THE-KNOT
www.theknot.com

Orbitz
Tel: 312/894-5000
www.orbitz.com

WeddingChannel.com
Tel: 888/750-1550
www.weddingchannel.com

Honeymoons, Inc.
Tel: 888/811-1888
www.honeymoonsinc.com

Spa Finder
Tel: 212/924-6800
www.spafinder.com

Destination Weddings

www.around-the-world.com

www.fijitravel.com

www.getawayweddings.com

www.resortvacationstogo.com

www.tropicaloccasions.com

All-inclusive honeymoons

www.beaches.com
Tel: 888/BEACHES

www.sandals.com
Tel: 888/SANDALS

Cruises

Tel: 888/CARNIVAL
www.carnival.com

Groom's added resources

Bliss Weddings
www.blissweddings.com

International Formalwear Association
www.formalwear.org

www.afterhours.com

Tuxedos and Formalwear by After Six,
Oscar de la Renta, and Seven Unlimited
www.aftersix.com

www.weddingspeech4u.com

Chapter Seven

Three Months To Go

If you're feeling scared, anxious, or unsettled as the Big Day approaches, try not to panic. This is a huge step you're taking, and it's natural—even expected—to find some doubts creeping in. There are many aspects of getting married that are frightening, but they only get worse if you try to hide them under a veil of false happiness. This is the chapter for you if your feet are starting to feel just the tiniest bit cold, or if your brain has suddenly started to focus on "What if?"

Pre-wedding doubts

Am so weird. Have been lying awake half the night worrying about getting married. Decided to write it down here to get it out and see if it makes sense. I'm so pleased to be marrying J., can't understand why bad thoughts keep creeping in. Not really bad thoughts either—not ones with any real foundation. Just dumb ones like: wives are frumpy. Much easier just to live with a man, then can leave any minute. Wives are forced to endure all kinds of trauma just for "sake of marriage." Is this true? No. Can still leave, indeed easier with $3,000 diamond ring to pawn for gas money.

Also worry that J. will have second thoughts. Don't expect him to—in fact, he has gotten nicer since engagement, sweeter, and more attentive. Making big effort, flowers, and so on. (Odd. Thought men relaxed after "getting" you?) But worried that he will start finding reasons to back out. Like, my thighs. Or my love of trashy TV. What was once endearing might become annoying when he realizes I'm his forever.

Such a scary word. I mean, I love J. and he is only man have ever considered marrying.

He makes me laugh, smile, think. Still surprises me with what he says. And he is sexiest man on planet. But marriage? Forever? Such a long time. See it stretching ahead, with no more dates. Aargh! I love dates. I was always good at dating. So no more dates? Ever? Frightening. Bit depressing, too. Know that good couples still make "dates" with each other after marriage, but that seems very forced.

Oh God. It's now 3:00 A.M. and I have to go shoe shopping tomorrow for wedding shoes. If don't get clear head and sleep soon, will break down and cry all over salesgirl. (Which, incidentally, did last week. Saw birthday card with photo of old couple snuggled up on bench by seaside. Lost it totally.)

So, let's get rational. Pros and cons of getting married:

Pros	Cons
J. all mine	Wives are frumpy
Everyone will know J. all mine	Sex life will vanish?
Relaxed—no dating anxiety	He HAS to be with me. Obligation
Living together. Bliss	No freedom. Can't just leave
Get to pamper him without looking like stalker girlfriend	Can't just book vacation for one (never did, but could want to)
Confirmation of his love for me	What if attracted to other men afterward?
Confidence-boosting	No more choice
Official "couple"	Decision made
Jewelry	

Aargh. Feeling no better and now 3:30 A.M. Do I need help? Should I call J.? Not great timing, but he should answer and talk to his Future Wife. No, can't call. Would look too odd.

How can you tell if nerves are real, if these are real reasons not to do it, or just cold feet? Jules said when she got married, she had panic attacks. In month before wedding, said she picked fights with Paul all time. Just to get reaction—to test him. Can understand, but not gone that bad yet. Like, want to see how committed he really is. Mom said she thinks J. is committed. Dad said he thinks J. should be committed, just for thinking about marrying me. Maybe true. Am not sanest girlfriend in world, so he must be keen to consider it. And he bought me this ring. AND he has told all friends and some exes about getting married. AND he EVEN likes me when I have no makeup on and wear his sweatpants. So, he likes me when I'm frumpy. Yes! The perfect man. Feel better. 'Night.

Deadlines for the countdown

◻ Send engagement announcements to newspapers and inform relatives.

◻ Reserve the venues (the earlier, the better) for the ceremony and the reception, and sign all relevant contracts.

◻ Meet your clergy member to discuss the ceremony and schedule pre-marital counseling if required by the church or synagogue.

◻ Consider writing your own vows or choose readings for the service.

◻ Meet the organist to determine appropriate music for the ceremony and discuss the addition of other musicians or vocalists.

◻ Arrange meetings with musical groups who can perform a range of tunes that will appeal to all at the reception and decide on music for the first dance. Enter into a contract that confirms the details.

◻ Invite your family, best friends, and relatives to be members of the wedding party. Discuss their attire and take measurements.

◻ Order the bridesmaids' dresses, confirming delivery for at least three weeks before the wedding to ensure enough time for alterations. (If the dresses are being made, the orders should be placed six months in advance.)

◻ Shop for accessories—shoes and jewelry for the women, ties and vests for the men—to complete their outfits.

◻ Help the mothers and grandmothers choose outfits and accessories. Invite the grandfathers to dress in the same style as the groomsmen and fathers.

◻ Schedule two dress fittings—one as soon as your dress arrives at the bridal shop and another about two weeks before the wedding.

◻ Make the preliminary menu choices with your caterer, selecting foods best suited for the season and time of day.

◻ Schedule appointments with several bakers to review their styles and workmanship. Choose one to produce the cake and place the order at least two months before the wedding.

◻ Interview several florists and review portfolios of their work. Identify your floral needs for the ceremony and reception, bouquets, and corsages.

Review the albums of several photographers to find the best professional. If you're going to video the wedding, arrange this as well, selecting any accompanying music you would like, and deciding how much of the day to cover.

Firm up the guest list. Order the invitations, "new home" cards, and thank-you notes.

Visit hotels near where the wedding will take place to suggest to out-of-town guests. Arrange for a discounted group rate and reserve a block of adjacent rooms if possible.

Arrange transportation to the ceremony and reception for the wedding party and immediate families.

Check on legal requirements for the marriage license. If you are marrying out of the country or out of state, complete any required paperwork.

Set up your bridal registry and select gifts with your fiancé.

Make reservations for the honeymoon.

Confirm the date and time of the rehearsal with those taking part.

> **"All my friends laughed at me when they saw the complex checklist I had devised for my wedding planning, but I swear it saved me from going crazy. I was religious about ticking off tasks as I completed them and it was fantastic to see the 'to do' list shrink as the Big Day approached."**
> **Sally, 22**

invitations

Allow three months before the wedding to order the invitations and prepare them for mailing. Always order more than you need in case you make mistakes or have last-minute add-ons.

If you need to, have place cards, response cards, "new home" cards, and thank-you notes printed at the same time, adapting your design to suit each.

Invitation style

The formality of your wedding should determine your choice of invitations. The most traditional ones are printed on white or ivory paper, folded on the left like a greeting card, and feature wording just on the top page. A popular variation places the wording in a paneled border or includes a personal insignia, while others are printed on handmade paper or on layered sheets affixed with a bow.

If you are having a super-coordinated theme for your day (see pages 24–25) you will want the invitations to capture the essence of that: bright sunshine colors for a tropical theme, printing on acetate instead of card for a wintry feel, and enclosing tiny sequin hearts for something more glitzy. With the wealth of art materials available—paper that is crinkly at the edges, foil-backed or studded with glitter, and pearly or metallic embossing paints—you can let your imagination run wild!

Once you have chosen the paper style, you'll need to select a font and decide whether you prefer engraving or thermography. Formal and semi-formal events typically call for a graceful, flowing script, while less formal weddings are better suited to a roman style.

If you want to veer away from tradition, consider sending a wedding invitation in postcard format, or including a gift with the invitation. Just keep in mind that the most important thing is that guests are aware of the details of the wedding and turn up at the right place on the right day!

Invitation wording

Since the details of any two weddings are never alike, the wording of invitations varies with each couple and the particulars of their individual celebration. There are no hard and fast rules, but a few conventions should help you decide what you want. It is usual to identify the hosts of the event—traditionally, the bride's family.

> *Mr. and Mrs. Roy Bowling*
> *request the pleasure of the company of*
> *(hand write guest's name)*
> *at the marriage of their daughter*
> *Madeline Claire to Mr. Lucas Duncan*
> *at the Holy Rosary Cathedral*
> *on Saturday, November 4, 2006*
> *at 3:00 P.M.*
> *Anytown, New York*

If your parents are divorced you have two options. The first is to combine the names of both parents on a single invitation. The second is to send separate invitations to the wedding, one hosted by the bride's mother and the other hosted by the bride's father. If sending one invitation, the bride's mother's name goes on the first line, whether she has remarried or not. The bride's father's name goes on the second line, without the "and."

When the couple is the host of the wedding, or when family ties are extended or complicated, something simpler is called for, as follows:

> *The honor of your presence*
> *is requested at the marriage of*
> *Miss Amy Michelle Callahan*
> *and*
> *Mr. Brian Anthony Evans*
> *on Saturday . . .*

Premarital counseling

It's not unusual for couples to hesitate about investing time in premarital counseling on the front end, but when they complete the sessions, they often find they have discovered numerous ways to strengthen their partnership.

More and more engaged couples are taking part in premarital counseling in order to build a strong foundation for married life together. In fact, it is not unusual for your celebrant—regardless of religion—to insist that you and your fiancé attend a series of classes or a weekend retreat before the wedding.

What are the benefits?

Participation in such a program is designed to help each of you understand your individual needs as well as those of the two of you as a couple. Typical subject areas include the way you'll interact with each other after the wedding and improving how you communicate with each other. You'll learn the necessity of balancing time alone and time together, and how to nurture yourself as well as your spouse. In addition to examining the nuances of speaking to each other and your respective families, you'll pay attention to developing better listening habits.

Above all, the sessions will help you gain awareness of the conflict that is inevitable to some degree in any partnership; and that it is perfectly normal for married couples to experience disagreements as they continue to grow together. Based upon your respective childhoods, each of you will have a preconceived idea of the perfect marriage and your role within it. You'll learn to "fight fair" in order to avoid the difficulties of "he said, she said," and to analyze what it is that each of you wants from the life ahead of you.

Through this counseling process, couples will recognize their attitudes toward many of the issues that challenge other married couples and their relationships, such as the handling of money and financial management, or the various issues surrounding pregnancy, parenting, and home life.

No doubt your celebrant will engage in a discussion on the role of religion in marriage and offer his or her assistance in helping the two of you to address conflicts that will arise over the course of years. Interfaith marriage is common today, and couples are taught how their upbringing may affect their relationship priorities, as well as strategies for having a healthy respect for each other's beliefs, whatever they are.

Finally, if either the bride or groom has been married previously, the counseling sessions will help to identify the difficulties in maintaining a happy union and how the two of you can strive to overcome whatever challenges lie ahead.

Family tensions

It's important to remember that a wedding is not just the union of bride and groom, but also the marriage of two families, and this inevitably means a further set of parents and siblings to consider when making your arrangements.

Regardless of how long you have known your future in-laws, there may be tension and anxiety that can strain relationships when planning a wedding. Those same feelings also hold true within your own family.

Armed with skills in diplomacy and a willingness to accept some compromises, engaged couples can help to avoid awkward and stressful encounters by being considerate of everyone's feelings. While traditional wedding etiquette can't solve all the personal conflicts, there are some guidelines that often smooth the stress and strain. But honest communication is the most essential component to keeping the peace.

There are a number of situations that might affect you, and it is best to be aware of them from the beginning, so that you can find ways of dealing with them when they come up.

There are countless brides who don't feel particularly close to their fiancé's sisters and so don't ask them to participate in the wedding party until some emotional eruption reveals their disappointment in not being asked. With a little creativity, you can always find ways to include your fiancé's family in the celebration.

An overbearing mother or future mother-in-law may want to be closely involved in planning the wedding details. Parents who are financially contributing to the wedding may feel that they should have a say. For other parents, the thought of "losing" a child and needing to share them with another family is threatening.

There may be relatives whom you simply don't care to invite. While receiving an invitation to your wedding should be considered an honor, recognize that you may cause ill feelings or perpetuate ongoing family tensions by not including certain people.

There may be step-parents and stepfamilies whose feelings are more important to you than those of blood relatives, in which case you will have to exercise a certain degree of diplomacy in having them involved.

Easing the tension

By anticipating everyone's emotions early in your planning, you should be able to avoid any incidents that might tarnish an otherwise perfect day.

You might start out by sharing the classic listing of who does what at a wedding to break the ice and determine their willingness and ability to satisfy the traditional checklist. Try to keep the contributions in line as you will want various expenses to remain in budget. Be tactful when it comes to building the guest list and arranging the reception seating. Make sure that divorced parents are surrounded with people they feel comfortable with.

Pay attention to the wording of your invitations, which will be influenced by the relationship between the bride to be's parents. Compatible terms can lead to both the mother and father of the bride to be extending the invitation.

If you anticipate any awkwardness among any of the immediate wedding party members, avoid a receiving line and just spend more time circulating among your guests after the ceremony.

Alert the photographer to any potential uneasiness. If you find yourself being photographed in a group that makes you feel a bit uncomfortable, be sure to smile and remember that you're not obliged to purchase every picture.

"I had a real struggle persuading Mom to come to my wedding, even though she and Dad have both had new partners for years. When she finally agreed, I knew I was going to have to be sensitive about seating arrangements, but did not want to feel totally beholden to her. I decided we would sit with her and Bob for the first two courses, and then we would swap seats with my maid of honor and her boyfriend so that we sat with Dad and Nancy for the rest of the meal and the toasts. Daisy, 34

Survival tactics

Don't doubt that there will be stressful moments along the way as all eyes are upon you and everyone seems to have an opinion about your Big Day…

Communicate: Don't be surprised if your fiancé is having a similar experience. The secret to keeping everything from spinning out of control is communication, honest and often, between the two of you and your families.

Remember your priorities: At any given stage of the planning process you will feel that there are a hundred and one details to take care of. Keep lists of the tasks at hand and prioritize to keep from becoming flustered.

Establish a routine: Set aside an hour at the same time each day to work on your wedding plans.

Get help: Delegate tasks to bridesmaids and family members. Your inner circle will become even closer, and you'll be relieved to get some of the responsibilities off your plate. Or, if you have the cash, hire a super-organized wedding planner.

Have a deadline: Make sure that the planning is over at least a week before your wedding, and slow down your activities as the Big Day approaches.

Get some sleep: Be sensible about what you can achieve in a day and go to bed at a reasonable hour. Sleep late on the day of the wedding, while allowing ample time for pampering.

Look after yourself: It's important not to forget good nutrition. Your metabolism needs to be in top condition for you to function properly, so make sure you eat a balanced diet and drink plenty of water, especially if you are exercising regularly.

Take a break: If it all gets to be too much, take some time out for a quick getaway for you and your fiancé. You'll come back feeling refreshed and ready to take up the reins again.

Stay positive: Remember that there is an end in sight to all the preparations you have been making, and nothing will stop you from getting there (eventually).

Resources

Premarital counseling

www.marriage.about.com/cs/
keysforsuccess/a/beginners.htm

www.marriagebuilders.com

www.premaritalonline.com

www.empathic.homestead.com

www.clairehatch.com/prewedding

Wedding vows

www.ultimatewedding.com

www.weddingsweddings.com

Stationery

www.paper-ya.com

www.weddingmagazine.com

www.bridestuff.com

www.laurapaladino.com
Tel: 866-265-0633

Wedding speeches

www.finespeeches.com

Chapter Eight

Two Months To Go

With just eight or so weeks to go, it must be coming up to the bachelorette party. How do you plan the perfect party—or how do you have your bridesmaids plan it for you? Should it be a lingerie party? A day at a spa? A meal at your favorite restaurant where you reminisce about the past and speculate about the future for Mrs. . . . or is it going to be Ms.? Are you going to change your name? Do you want to? What does your fiancé think? Don't worry about a thing—this chapter has it all, plus a list of everything you need to get done this month to keep your wedding on track.

Dear Diary,

Expectations for the bachelorette party

Have moral dilemma. How can I word the bachelorette party invitations without sounding like I'm basically saying, "please buy me presents?" Of course that IS what I'm saying. . . . And everyone'll know . . . But still . . .

Really want a wild night out with the girls. Thinking back to some of the parties I've attended, the greatest have been when we all go away for a whole weekend. Jules's was awesome—we rented a luxury boat and went sailing off the coast. We didn't have to do anything, except lie on the deck sipping champagne. Heaven. That's what I'd love. It was expensive though—and everyone I know is broke.

Other ideas: weekend in Vegas? Dancing, nightclubs, me dressed up in big white fake veil—no. Weekend at health spa: beauty treatments, manicures, leg waxing, bikini waxing, spots breaking out, allergic reactions, looking like burns victim on wedding day—no. Very civilized dinner near home, back by 11 P.M., no dancing, just mature conversation—no.

Aargh! What can I do? Could have a party at my apartment . . . Maybe . . . But lot of hassle just before wedding. Plus have to move out of here in next couple of months and a party will mean more cleaning. Anita is keen to arrange something, but it's all being held up by my not knowing what I want. She says she'd prefer a quiet evening, if it were her party. But she's more of a homebody than me. I want a riotous time. Hmm.

Talking to J. earlier about his bachelor party. His best man has arranged it, and it's a day of golf, then some go-kart racing, then a dinner. There'll be about seven of them. Sounds good.

This is stupid but . . . I want to have as good a time. Don't want to be doing something yawnsome if HE'S going to be going crazy. Don't think he'll have strippers, but never know. Don't trust his best man at ALL. Anything could happen.

Done. A. has booked a weekend in the wine country! Six of us: me and A., Emma, Jules, Liz, and Bill (counts as woman

'cause he's gay). We're staying in a pretty hip B&B (top-of-the-line) and they have offered us a deal because it's out of season. There are a couple of clubs and loads of bars. So we can have everything: wine-tasting, drinking, dancing, and some fun. Plus L. is going to bring loads of beauty stuff to give us all treatments, and B. has learned how to read tarot cards.

Of course, I will not kiss anyone. I don't mean the girls or B. I mean strangers. On TV last night was drama about woman who met ex-boyfriend while out partying week before her wedding, and dumped fiancé within three hours. All very exciting and passionate, but unlikely for me. For one thing, only men likely to meet on my bachelorette weekend are jerks. Mmmmmm. Hold me back!

Writing this after no sleep for three days. Ugh. Not drinking again till wedding, if ever. What happened to quiet weekend A. promised me? B. is in state of shock—said he never knew girls were so predatory and he's glad he's gay.

Went out Sat. night to bar in town. Was quiet and we would have gone home had a local baseball team not arrived. They were all drunk and said we all looked gorgeous! They knew of a party, and after 0.4 seconds' contemplation, we decided to join them. Was in nearby house—very studenty. But loads of booze. I mean LOADS. The bath was full of ice and beer. (Woke up next A.M. with bottle of vodka down bra.)

Had relatively quiet time, but E., L., and B. got very drunk. E. ended up kissing captain under tarp-covered boat in driveway and L. almost got in fight with other player's girlfriend.

Got back to hotel at seven to find the keys in room door and L. asleep on sofa!

Ugh. J. asked me for details and I lied a little. Said was very quiet, let's-try-new-hairstyles sort of thing. Partly hate that it sounds so dull, but mainly long for peace and quiet and a month's sleep. Hope will recover before Big Day. Eek—gotta go . . . Eugh . . .

Deadlines for the countdown

This is where your planning skills really come to the front. You should be well on the way to finalizing most of the critical aspects of the day, and remember—an ounce of organization now is worth a pound of panic on the day.

- Create your own system or spreadsheet to keep track of the guest list, invitations, gifts received, and thank-you notes written.
- Mail the invitations six weeks before the wedding. Those being sent to another country should be mailed at least eight weeks in advance.
- Double-check that the celebrant, bridesmaids, groomsmen, and all others involved in the ceremony are available.
- Pick out the wedding bands and specify any desired engraving.
- Make appointments with your hairdresser to have your hair trimmed two to three weeks before the wedding, to have a trial run, and for the Big Day.
- Assess the need for baby-sitting services or special activities for the young children of your bridal party members and guests.
- Invite close relatives and special friends not in the wedding party to perform honored tasks on the day.
- Purchase special gifts for members of the wedding party. Look for items that can be personalized with names and the date of the celebrations.
- Find a service to preserve your wedding bouquet, and request a "toss bouquet" from your florist to toss when you leave the reception.
- Purchase any accessories, such as the ring-bearer's pillow, a guest book, toasting goblets, and cake knife.
- Schedule a tasting of the wedding meal for about six weeks before the wedding so that there is enough time to make minor changes.
- Schedule a tasting with your cake baker to decide on the cake and icing flavors, and design the top tier to preserve.
- Check there will be reserved parking spaces outside the ceremony and obtain any necessary parking permits.
- Buy new luggage if you need it.
- Schedule physical examinations for each of you and arrange for any immunizations required for your honeymoon travel plans.

What's in a name?

As your wedding approaches, you will need to decide whether or not to change your surname. You are not legally obliged to do so, and there are pros and cons with both options.

Until the 1970s, it was common for brides to take their new husband's last name as their surname. Today, however, more and more brides are giving significant thought to the choices they have in selecting a name that they'll use for the rest of their life.

What are your options?

You can change your maiden name to your husband's surname.

You can keep your maiden name as a middle name, or hyphenate it with your husband's to create a new surname. (Your husband may wish to use this new name as well.)

You can keep your maiden name or use it for your professional life, while taking your husband's surname for all other situations.

Your husband can take your maiden name as his surname.

Things to consider

If you have established a professional identity, changing your name may cause confusion. If you are the last descendant to carry your family name, you might feel it is a shame to lose it. Does your fiancé support your choice? Will your decision work in the future, especially if you have children?

Changing Your Name

If you take your husband's name, you must change your name on all of your personal and business records as well. Contact the Department of Social Security, your vehicle licensing bureau, your bank, accountant, and any other professional with whom you do business.

Bridal showers & bachelorette parties

The bridal shower is a long-held custom where friends of the engaged woman "shower" her with gifts for her dowry. This is the only part of the entire process where you can openly indulge in receiving lots of great gifts. Enjoy!

Shower etiquette

Invitations to a shower should be mailed about four weeks in advance of the party, and usually friends or relatives host the event. Two showers or more are considered greedy, although it is possible to bend this rule when the guests at each get-together are a different crowd.

Showers are primarily characterized by a theme around a particular group of gifts, and are usually organized around afternoon tea or an evening at home. For example, the hostess may choose an area of your home to furnish, like the kitchen. Another popular idea is a lingerie shower, where guests bring items of underwear for the bride (and groom!) to enjoy on the honeymoon.

Bachelorette parties

Bachelorette parties celebrate the passage from singlehood to marriage. These parties can range from the tame to the extreme, depending upon the personality of the bride. Popular choices are to have dinner in a favorite restaurant, a day at the beach, a night of clubbing, or a spa weekend.

> "My fiancé wanted to keep our honeymoon a secret but I was frustrated because I needed some idea about what to pack. So he got together with my maid of honor and all the gifts at my shower were for the honeymoon. They gave me sunscreen, a snorkel, and flippers! I didn't know the destination, but I had a good idea of the kind of vacation I was getting. **Charlotte, 37**

Gifts for the attendants

Many brides and grooms buy gifts for their attendants. Traditionally, these are presented at the rehearsal, on the morning of the wedding, or during the speeches at the reception.

Some brides and grooms choose an identical item for each attendant—perhaps personalized with the date of the wedding or the recipient's initials—while others choose more individual gifts. If the gift is an accessory to complete a wedding day outfit the recipient should receive it by the morning of the wedding at the very latest.

For the girls

Traditional: jewelry set, jewelry box, picture frame, compact or hand mirror, engraved letter opener.
Personal: perfume, personalized journal, bracelet, charm, book.

For the boys

Traditional: silk vest for wedding outfit, pen, grooming kit, cuff links, watch.
Personal: tie, monogrammed handkerchiefs, cologne, box of cigars.

❝When Charlie and Amanda got married we knew they were bound to do something different. They had a movie theme and each guest came as his or her favorite character from a film. The happy couple dressed up as John Travolta and Uma Thurman in *Pulp Fiction*. They looked amazing. When it came to gifts for the attendants, all the boys got pump-action water pistols and the girls had little black wigs and scarlet lipstick.   **Trish, 34**

Survival tactics

A bachelorette party or shower can present a whole host of awkward situations and embarrassments. Whatever you are planning, it pays to bear a couple of typical pitfalls in mind:

Bridesmaids' burden

It is likely that your bridesmaids will be included as guests at every event in your honor, and this could turn into a financial burden for them. If you want to avoid potential animosity, discreetly mention that you look forward to them joining in the festivities and request that they don't feel obliged to bring gifts.

Be sensible

For many brides to be, like ours, the bachelorette party turns into an unpleasant memory if there is too much alcohol or wildness. Make sure you choose the right person to arrange your party, someone you can rely on to keep things under control.

Don't worry, be happy

Whether or not you are party to the adventure planned for your groom, don't waste time or energy worrying how his evening might be going. Leave your fears at home and make the most of your own rite of passage.

Thank you

Amid the thank-you letters that follow your engagement and the ones for wedding gifts that arrive before the Big Day, it is easy to forget to thank people for the shower and bachelorette party and any gifts. Ask the hostess to keep track of each gift and giver and present you with a final list.

Resources

Wedding favors

Pretty Accents
Tel: 330/309-9746
www.prettyaccents.com

WeddingAccessories.net
www.weddingaccessories.net

Wedding Tulle
www.weddingtulle.com

Beaucoup Wedding Favors
Tel: 877/988-BEAU
www.beau-coup.com

Wedding Things
Tel: 888/338-8818
www.weddingthings.com

www.myweddingfavors.com

Wedding accessories and attendants' gifts

www.cathysconcepts.com

www.americanbridal.com

www.weddingdepot.com

www.wedding-presents.com

www.weddingshowergifts.com

Wedding Registries

www.aperfectweddinggift.com

www.thebigday.com

www.bridaltips.com

www.theknot.com

www.target.com/gp/gift-registries.html

www.weddingchannel.com

Changing your name

www.bridelaw.com

www.uslegalforms.com

Chapter Nine
One Month To Go

Can you believe it? In less than a month it'll all be over. You've come so far that you might be tempted to relax and kick back this month. Don't be fooled. There's still a list of chores for you to do. But don't worry—getting busy is the best way to keep last-minute nerves at bay. In addition to the deadlines for this month, you'll find advice on the odd contingency plan for if (when) something goes wrong.

The rehearsal

Well, THAT was calming! There's nothing like a wedding rehearsal to get you going. Off at the deep end, that is. Just got back, and J. is here too, being an absolute angel and making me nightcap and running a bath for me. (Aaah.) But anyway, the rehearsal. . . It was so funny.

We all turned up at the vineyard this afternoon, just after lunch. Mom and Dad were beaming and really excited. Anita and Nick were both worried about what they had to do when and if they'd fall over/giggle/accidentally marry each other. J. was calm as anything, but I was stressed because my pre-wedding haircut had gone wrong. My bangs are SO short. I look like I've grown an extra two inches of forehead . . . So not my wedding vision. Couldn't concentrate on anything, until they all went into the stables and Dad, A., and I were left outside.

Got a little tearful. When the music started and the waiter opened the door, all I could see was J. standing at the end of the room waiting for me. Just wanted to run up to him (hmm, will I ever learn to play it cool?), but Dad insisted we do the proper, slow wedding march. Sloooowly. So slowly that I got the giggles, which set Mom off, too. Dad got a little grumpy then.

The celebrant went over the vows really quickly, and I was very relieved that I didn't have much to say. It's not like a church wedding: the vows are very brief. All we say is, "I give you this ring as a token of my love," something about not knowing any reason why we can't lawfully marry, and a couple of "I do's." And that's it.

N. read out the poem we're having and deliberately messed up for laughs. He's threatening to cough during that part of the service where the celebrant asks if anyone knows a reason why we can't marry. A tiny part of me sort of hopes that an ex will appear and stand in the aisle, screaming, "Kaaaaaate!" (like in *The Graduate*), but I don't know anyone who's that devoted. Even R., who felt "physically sick" when I told him I was engaged, is now dating someone else. Schmuck. Why don't men carry torches anymore? Am I so easy to get over?

J. got mushy after the rehearsal and said that it was really starting to sink in now. What? He's cutting it a little close! But I know what he means. Up until now it's been a little like a dream, or planning a party. Going through it today has really made it "real." Asked him if he was having second thoughts and he was great—he said he'd never had a moment's doubt from the day we met . . . just months and months of them. Which was almost the loveliest thing anyone's ever said to me. Almost.

All went out to dinner afterward. J.'s Mom booked table at fabulous Italian restaurant. Not just the wedding party, but a ton of J.'s relatives too—all staying nearby, so quite a crowd. Really loved it, such a relief after the stress of the rehearsal. Mom and Dad seemed to kick back a little too. All having such a good time that no one minded me and J. leaving before dessert. Wanted to get back for some quiet time together (his idea, not mine, wonder what he has in mind . . .).

Actually, still have loads to do. I've been packing up my stuff to move out. That brings it home. I've had such a good time in my single-girl pad. Dinner parties, dates, sleepover parties. . . When I think of leaving, I get a little upset. Had such a great time here. And this is the apartment where J. and I had our first kiss, out in the hallway. That still makes me tingle to think of it. This is where he first tried to wrestle my top off me on our second date, to no avail. This is where I played hard to get on the third—and where I eventually gave in, on the sixth. I've cooked him dinner here (and burned it), I've served him cocktails (and spilled them), and I've even made him a birthday cake (got the number of candles wrong!). It's the apartment he's arrived at so many times, carrying flowers and champagne and presents . . . It's also where he told me he loved me. Sniff!

Got to stop thinking like that or I'll never leave. Must go and see if J. needs any help in the kitchen, and if his top needs wrestling off . . .

Deadlines for the countdown

If anything is likely to go wrong, it will be in the last few weeks before the wedding. In addition to taking care of the finishing touches for the day—sorting out your beauty arrangements, choosing a gift for your fiancé—make sure you keep close tabs on all the pros and stay excited!

- Set up a meeting at your church or synagogue to determine the logistical procedures, including where you and the wedding party can dress before the ceremony and where the flowers should be delivered.
- Revisit the site with the photographer and videographer, and review your requests.
- Double-check the reception site's policy on tossing confetti, rice, or petals.
- Ask the caterer to pack a picnic basket for you and your husband to take when you leave the reception.
- Choose a personal gift for your fiancé that can be presented during a private moment together.
- Decide on the favors for guests at the reception.
- Purchase a supply of umbrellas if the weather forecast suggests there will be rain on the Big Day. Choose a particularly pretty one for yourself!
- Consult a makeup artist about your wedding day look and test new cosmetics.

Spend a pampering day at the beauty salon with your bridesmaids, enjoying massages, manicures, and pedicures.

Collect passports, visas, and traveler's checks for the honeymoon. Assemble receipts for the airline tickets, car rental, hotel reservations, and any excursion packages.

Make a list of the bills that will be due on the Big Day, adding appropriate tips.

Open joint bank accounts and determine how you will handle them and pay bills.

Check with your home owner's insurance to confirm that your wedding gifts are going to be adequately protected, and review your joint insurance policies to take in account of your new circumstances.

Notify each of your employers and/or your insurance agent(s) of your upcoming marriage and the need to name your new spouse as the beneficiary of any life insurance policy.

Consult with a lawyer to name each other the beneficiaries in your wills.

Complete all the necessary documents to change your name, if you are doing so.

Keep up with writing thank-you notes for the multitude of gifts and well wishes that arrive at this time.

The wedding rehearsal

Typically, in the week leading up to the wedding—even on the last day—all of the attendants and immediate family members will meet with the celebrant for a run through of the ceremony. Everyone will learn where he or she is supposed to stand and when he or she is supposed to move.

This is a great opportunity for you both to see the wedding as an onlooker. As the bride, your best vantage point may be toward the back watching the ritual unfold as your guests will on the day. Do you approve of the placement of members of the wedding party? The pace of the processional and recessional? Is the volume of the music okay?

Take whatever time is necessary for everyone to practice the ceremony process, and if there are children in the wedding party, try to keep them focused.

It's vitally important for you to have the opportunity of walking to music. And don't forget to practice handing your bouquet to your maid of honor when you reach the altar. At the end, take back your flowers, reach for your groom's arm, or clasp hands, and practice taking your first steps as newlyweds.

Be sure to introduce everyone—especially those groomsmen and bridesmaids that will be matched for the recessional. It might help to think through the pairing of bridesmaids and groomsmen before the rehearsal, rather than bumbling through this during the rehearsal. Think about which attendants will get along well with each other and avoid pairing a couple that look mismatched when they are walking together.

This may be the first time many of the people involved in different aspects of your wedding come together, so it can be the perfect opportunity—as our bride to be found—to arrange a get-together after the rehearsal. Keep it informal, but offering a few toasts to special relatives and friends who are playing big roles, is bound to be appreciated. Consider holding it at a restaurant close to the rehearsal site, in order to make it as easy as possible for everyone important to make it.

Contingencies

Let's face it. At some point, something is bound to go wrong. By recognizing this possibility in advance and making plans for some swift alternatives, you can avert disaster—and no one need know how close calamity was.

As the wedding day approaches

Stay in regular contact with the professionals who are providing services for the day. Top professionals can experience a blunder in their business, but they should also have contingency plans of their own.

Although disruption will be tedious, there is very little that cannot be remedied. Only you know what you were expecting and your guests will be unaware of any last-minute changes.

When it comes to what you and your wedding party are wearing, however, it can take strength of character to overcome a disaster. If you're worried about your gown's fit, schedule a fitting about a week before the wedding and be prepared to pay for the rapid turnaround service. And stay on top of the delivery of the bridesmaids' gowns.

On the day of your wedding

Get someone to visit the ceremony and reception sites to check that the flowers have arrived, the cake is where it should be, and so on. They can also make confirming telephone calls to the band, photographer, and so on.

> ❝I had gotten so wrapped up in the planning that I was obsessed with every tiny detail. One of the bridesmaid's dresses came with a mistake in the embroidery and I completely lost it. I think all the nervous energy building up finally came out in one huge outburst. I made a real fool of myself. **Stephanie, 28**

Survival tactics

If you find it difficult keeping calm in the face of pending disaster, just remind yourself of the complexity of your planning process and congratulate yourself on getting so much right.

Rest assured that you will know at an early stage whether one supplier or another is going to be reliable or not. Trust your instinct and be firm in your instruction. If you have serious concerns about getting what you want from a professional, find someone else. You cannot afford to give anyone the benefit of the doubt.

When you are looking for suppliers first time around, keep the contact details of all your second choices, and put them somewhere that is easy to find. In most cases it will be a simple phone call that saves the day.

Don't rely on suppliers to keep you informed. Double-check their deadlines and make sure they come through. As a rule, do not let anything slip more than five days. If they do, have no shame in chasing them relentlessly.

Remember you are not alone in this, particularly as the day gets nearer. If something goes wrong, call up your fiancé, your mother, or a bridesmaid for support. A problem shared . . .

Once you get to the day before the wedding, make final confirmations and similar jobs someone else's responsibility. Chances are you won't even know about any eleventh-hour dilemmas, which is how it should be.

If a supplier really lets you down on the day, remain calm, take it in stride, and do not let it spoil your wedding. You can take it up with them when you get back from your honeymoon.

Resources

Wedding day transportation

National Limousine Association
Tel: 800/652-7007
www.nlaride.com

www.limousines.com

Preserving your gown

www.fabriclink.com

www.a-weddingday.com/

www.ehow.com

Bridal garters

www.alfawedding.com

www.weddingaccessories.net

Thank-you notes

www.bridalguide.com

www.weddingusa.com

Wedding dance lessons

www.1greatdancesite.com

www.youshouldbedancing.com

Honeymoon packing tips

www.honeymoonlocation.com

www.honeymoons-by-sunset.com

Wedding tosses

www.weddingpetals.coom

www.weddingrice.com

Chapter Ten
One Week To Go

Everything is arranged and all there is time for now is a last-minute panic. Do
you have time for that? Of course not! So here's how to keep cooler than the
proverbial cucumber. We have everything you need to allay your fears, from
long, hot herbal baths for beating stress, to mantras you can repeat as you sail
up the aisle. You'll find your final checklists for deadlines here, as well as a
wedding day timetable to keep things on track.

Pre-wedding tremors

So this is it. I'm getting married tomorrow. From tomorrow, I'll be married. I'll be a Mrs. No more Miss. I'll officially belong to someone. I'll be betrothed. I'll be able to tell old wives' tales ('cause I'll be an old wife). I'll have a husband. I'll be able to tell plumbers and car mechanics, "You'll have to deal with my husband." I'll have a wedding ring that'll stop me ever being chatted up again—bah. But I'll be able to have sex whenever I like—yay. I'm really excited. I'm really scared. I'm absolutely, positively sure I'm doing the right thing, but I don't really know.

Absolutely everything is arranged now. My dress is hanging up on the closet door—Mom put it there so it's the first thing I see when I wake up (cheesy, but I like it). I've spent today in the little beauty salon around the corner, having my nails done and eyebrows shaped. (Should have done that years ago—it looks great.) All the bachelorette party girls came, even Bill, though we had to stop him from having Botox injections. My legs are shaved, my makeup is laid out on the dressing table. Anita and Becky are downstairs with Mom, Dad, and Nick, and my honeymoon suitcase is packed and ready to go beside my bed.

How do I feel? Weirdly calm . . . With bouts of hysteria. Can't stop smiling, and waves of happiness, joy, and delight keep taking me by surprise at the oddest moments. I'm pleased to be getting married, actually doing it—it feels like I've been "chosen." I don't have to be a singleton any more, a one-woman band. From now on there'll be two of us to shoulder things.

I'm also nervous, in case it goes wrong. Not the day—there are loads of people to fix problems at the vineyard, and A. is being awesome about shielding me from stress. But I'm scared that the marriage will go wrong in one, three, maybe ten years' time—but then again, I'm sure it won't. How can it? It's weird. I'm in a daze, really. A can't-believe-it, this-is-all-a-dream, how-did-I-get-here daze.

I'll miss being engaged. That sounds so lame, but I will. Engagement is easy—it's all roses and flowers and diamonds. It's whirlwind excitement, and kissing, and laughter. Marriage doesn't have the same promise . . . I'm scared it'll be all broken washing machines and nagging and TV-watching. I so want to be a good wife. I want to look pretty every day, be calm and in control, to cook apple pies and dumplings (without ever getting fat), and be supportive and kind to J. I want to be the ultimate homemaker, and beautiful.

My main fear, of course, is that, after everything we have been through, J. won't turn up tomorrow morning. Naturally. He's at home tonight, with his parents. We've spoken already today and his suit is ready, he's had a haircut, and he's put gas in the car. Tomorrow he's got to drive a fair distance to the vineyard so—obviously—I'm worried sick that he'll crash before I can get to him. I'm scared his alarm won't go off. I'm scared it will, but then he'll decide not to come. I'm scared . . .

I'm just scared. This is such a big step. It's really hitting me now. But I'll still go through with it. Oh—text message! It's from J. No! Is this it then? Do people call off weddings via text message these days? I had a friend who told her fiancé by email—spineless I thought. It'd be very modern, though. Very 21st century.

Hang on, it says—"Can't wait for tomorrow. I love you more than anything and you'll be the best wife in the world. Too excited to sleep XXX. P.S. Don't be late!"
Aaaaah.

Deadlines for this week

Pretty much everything should be in place now, with all the final arrangements coming together as planned. All that is left for you to do is apply yourself to the finishing touches, and make sure everyone else knows what they are doing!

- Try on your wedding gown and headpiece for the last time before the wedding and assemble it with the undergarments, shoes, and jewelry.

- Confirm that the formalwear shop is delivering all the men's attire to where they should be on the morning of the wedding.

- Touch base with your clergy member to be sure everything is in order for the ceremony. Make copies of the readings to give to the attendants.

- Tally up the guest response cards and add in the number of members of the wedding party to determine a final head count.

- Confirm all the food and beverage details with the caterer, and provide the total number of attendees at the reception.

- Confirm all the details with the florist, including delivery of flowers to the ceremony and reception venues. Arrange for the mothers' and

grandmothers' flowers and fathers' and grandfathers' boutonnieres to be delivered to where they will dress for the wedding.

Confirm the wedding cake delivery and set-up times with the baker. Be sure that any family keepsakes used as decoration will be returned to you after the wedding.

Anticipate the toasts and/or speeches you and your new husband will want to offer at the reception, and finalize notes.

Wrap the gifts for the members of the wedding party.

Remind both sets of parents of who stands where in the receiving line at the reception, if you are having one.

Put away any wedding gifts already received in your new home so that you're ready to relax comfortably when you return from the honeymoon.

Make up the bed in your new home with soft sheets and lots of pillows. Stock the refrigerator with wine and snacks for a romantic feast.

Double-check the paperwork required by the celebrant.

Start packing for the honeymoon!

Last-minute jitters

Overwhelmed as the complexity of all the details and mounting stress hits a peak just before the Big Day? Even the most level-headed bride will have a panic attack or two, so it's important to have a vehicle for relieving anxieties.

If you're not sleeping soundly and are snapping at those around you, or have lost your appetite AND sense of humor, it's time to back off and employ some mood-enhancement strategies. (In most cases, you just need a temporary escape to regain your balance, but don't hesitate to talk with your physician if you have more serious concerns.)

You're probably watching what you eat to be sure you fit into your dress, but you need plenty of food and water. Don't deprive yourself of food cravings, but try to keep them in moderation. Cut back on high-caffeine drinks and replace them with herbal tea or fruit juices.

Try to get at least eight hours sleep per night. If your sleep quotient is off track, take advantage of the odd quiet moment and power nap.

A massage or aromatherapy treatment might cure general aches, while a manicure and pedicure will pamper. Although you'll be as busy as ever in the last weeks, try to keep up with your exercise regimen or at least do some walking or stretching every day. Gentle yoga and proper breathing techniques, for example, can help you maintain physical flexibility and stay calm.

Light some scented candles and run a bath. Add a few drops of your favorite essential oils to help you relax.

Make time to curl up with a good book or listen to your favorite music. Or take possession of the remote control and tune in to your favorite show.

Stay connected with your friends and don't be shy about sharing your emotions with them as well as your fiancé.

Employ some delegating strategies to people you can totally depend on to help lighten the load on your shoulders.

One day to go

This is it. There is no turning back and all you can do now is enjoy yourself. Try to relax and accept that anything that hasn't been done by the end of the day won't be done and cannot be important.

Final countdown

Here is your last set of deadlines:

- Deliver the orders of service to a trusted family member or friend to pass out at the marriage ceremony.

- Prepare the celebrant's fee or make a contribution to your church or synagogue in his or her honor.

- Double-check with the ushers to be sure that they are clear on where family members and guests are to be seated.

- Share the spotlight at a bridesmaids' luncheon. Present your attendants' gifts then, if you like.

- Write a special thank-you note to both sets of parents from the two of you to express your appreciation for their love and support throughout your engagement. Arrange for it to be delivered with flowers.

- Go to bed early for plenty of rest the night before the wedding!

The Big Day

Congratulations! You made it. You are going to be a bride. All the hard work that has gone into the planning over the last half-year or so will pay off today.

The best advice for any bride to be is to sleep as late as possible on your wedding day. Not only will you need the rest to fuel the energy you'll be burning throughout the day, but a good night's sleep will soften the under-eye circles that signal too many late nights. Even if you're not a big breakfast eater, give your stomach some nourishment right away and graze until the time to start dressing for the wedding on a bunch of mini-meals.

Your wedding countdown

Below is a sample wedding day timetable to give you an idea of what should happen when so that you can keep things on track.

Five hours to go

Shower and dress casually in a button-up shirt so as not to ruin your hair and makeup later. While you are waiting for the hair and makeup stylists to arrive, glance over your packing list and tuck any last-minute items into your honeymoon suitcase.

Four hours to go

Your hair stylist should arrive and can start arranging your hair as discussed in your earlier sessions.

Three hours to go

Your bouquet and the corsages for the wedding party will arrive. The makeup artist should arrive around this time, along with the other women in the wedding party. Enjoy the pampering as your makeup is applied. Sit back while the nail technician adds a protective topcoat to your manicure and pedicure.

Two hours to go

You should make time to break for something to eat before getting into your outfit. The photographer should arrive shortly, if he or she has not been with you all morning, and will begin to take photos of you and the female wedding party getting ready and in formal groups.

At around this time the flowers will be arranged at the church and reception sites, the caterer will be overseeing both the meal preparation and the setting of the reception tables, and the baker will be adding finishing touches to the decoration of the wedding cake.

One hour and 45 minutes to go

The photographer will leave and make his or her way to the groom's house to take pictures of him and his groomsmen as they leave for the ceremony site. The florist should arrive with the boutonnieres.

One hour to go

The limousines will arrive at both the bride's and groom's homes.

45 minutes to go

The mother of the bride and bridesmaids leave the bride's house. The groom and his party leave the groom's house.

30 minutes to go

The groom and best man take their places inside, and remain seated at the front. The ushers and groomsmen will greet the guests who will have begun arriving at the church and escort them to their seats.

15 minutes to go

The bride and her father depart. On arrival at the ceremony site, the wedding director will help the group to settle and the photographer will take photographs of you and your bridesmaids before the start of the ceremony.

The celebrant will come to each group to check everything is in order and offer a short prayer and blessing. You'll get ready to take your place at the entrance to the chapel.

The ceremony

The processional music begins. You make your way up the aisle and begin the ceremony. At around this time, the baker will be delivering the cake and setting up at the reception site, as will the musicians.

Survival tactics

A wedding day is like no other day of your life. For this one day you are going to be the center of attention and will probably be feeling charged with energy and emotion. Most brides say their wedding day goes by in a flash, but it is a long day and you should be prepared for it.

An empty stomach, or one filled with the wrong types of food, can play havoc with your nerves. Avoid anything very fatty or high in sugar, and pass on the carbonated drinks. Instead get plenty of water inside you and have a light meal before leaving for the ceremony.

It goes without saying that you should take it easy the night before the Big Day. Too much alcohol will leave you feeling groggy and smoking before you go to bed may disrupt your sleep. Limit your caffeine intake on the morning, and if the champagne is flowing, go easy on it, or avoid it until you get to the reception.

Make sure you leave enough time to pamper yourself. Take a long bath first thing and have the hair stylist and makeup artist arrive with plenty of time so they can work in a relaxed manner. You don't want to leave for the ceremony feeling stressed out.

If you have a blemish on the day (and it can happen) whatever you do, don't make it worse. Use a medicated ointment to dry it out (toothpaste and vodka have been known to work, too) and have your makeup artist deal with it for you.

Try to steal quiet moments to yourself as you prepare, even if this means locking yourself in the bathroom for five minutes of deep breathing.

Repeat a mantra as a quick and effective form of mind control. If you know you are going to get jittery as you walk up the aisle, think of something you can be saying in time with your steps.

Dear Diary,

Happily ever after

We've done it! I'm now officially J.'s and he's officially mine. There's a piece of paper to prove it and everything. No one has called me Mrs. yet, but when J. and I were checking in at the hotel, he put his arm around me and said something about his wife to the woman at reception and I could see him nearly explode with pride. (It is so nice that he is so happy to be married to me!)

Don't know now why I was so scared before the wedding—he was there when I arrived (of course—no accident on the way to the service) and when I walked down the aisle with Dad, I saw him brush away a little tear from his cheek. Mom, of course, was bawling. When I was only a few steps away from J., we sort of locked eyes, and I really can't remember much of the rest of the service—just that neither one of us messed up the vows, and then all of a sudden we were married!

I can't believe how much my face hurts from all the smiling! There was a grin on my face from the moment I walked into the church until we left the party just before midnight. I was tempted to hit the photographer over the head with his camera around 8.00 P.M., but I remembered that we needed shots of the dancing, so I held back.

The stable where we had the reception looked amazing! There was one little disaster when Anita knocked over her red wine during dinner (it missed my dress by about an inch!), but the staff were so quick to replace the tablecloth that no one really noticed and A. climbed out from under the table where she was sitting, very, very embarrassed. But of course, she was brave enough to accept another glass!

I think my favorite part of the day though was when J. and I were driven off to have some photos taken between the wedding and the reception. We got to have a little time to ourselves (if

you don't count the photographer and driver) and J. told me again how much he loved me and how happy he is to be married to me, and how beautiful I looked. J. gave me some lovely earrings to match my engagement ring. I wanted to cry but didn't want my mascara to run, so I settled on a long, soft kiss instead— so much easier to reapply the lipstick before the next round of photos! I gave him a watch that I knew he'd adore, engraved on the back with the date we met and the date of the wedding, and he put it on right away.

It feels nice (and a little weird) to hold hands with him now and feel our wedding rings knock together, but these are the little things that I'm looking forward to now that we are married and can start living happily ever after.

We're leaving some stuff (like the dress and suit) here for Mom and Dad to pick up later, and we're off this morning to Hawaii—I can't wait to relax on the beach with a cocktail, take long walks hand in hand with the waves breaking around our feet, and spend long hours looking into each other's eyes as the sun sets over the hills . . . all the stress leading up to the wedding has been more than worth it. Must go, or we'll be late for our flight . . .

index